Gospel

Gospel in Esther

Michael Beckett

May this woman inspire you
as she inspired me

Michael Beckett

PATERNOSTER PRESS

Published 2002 by Paternoster Press

08 07 06 05 04 03 02   7 6 5 4 3 2 1

Paternoster Press is an imprint of Authentic Media,
PO Box 300, Carlisle, Cumbria, CA3 0QS, UK
and Box 1047, Waynesboro, GA 30830-2047, USA
www.paternoster-publishing. com

British Library Cataloguing in Publication Data
A catalogue record for this book is available from the British Library

ISBN 1-84227-137-7

Cover by FourNineZero
Typeset by Westkey Ltd, Falmouth, Cornwall
Printed in Great Britain by Cox and Wyman, Reading, Berkshire

Contents

Foreword

Esther as a type of Jesus? The mere proposal seems absurd to anyone who has recently read this short story of 'sexual politics, violence, vengeance, political intrigue and murder', as Michael Beckett appropriately describes it.

But, of course, the Book of Esther is part of a series of Old Testament stories of redemption, of the deliverance of the people of Israel from enslavement in a foreign land. To eyes enlightened by the final deliverance brought about by Jesus, modes of interpretation are opened up, for which the gaps of centuries, of context and of gender cease to be insurmountable obstacles.

This book is the fruit of a course of sermons delivered in a Cambridge parish church long noted for its attentiveness to the work of preaching. It is an up-to-date example of a very traditional kind of biblical interpretation, now called 'theological exegesis'. The basic motivation of those who gathered the books of Holy Scripture together was the conviction that in them may be read God's ways with humankind. To share that conviction enables us to overcome the 'tyranny of distance' that apparently separates us from vastly different cultures. If on the one hand the Book of Esther strikes us as 'an amusing tale of political intrigue and sexual power play', on the other it is precisely in such grubby contemporary circumstances that God is bringing about the work of redemption and liberation among us. We are no longer oppressed by the pessimistic thought that the passage of time has placed an impenetrable barrier between Esther's day and ours. Suddenly, to the eye of faith, there is a great deal to discover through a careful re-reading of this book.

It is striking to me that Michael encourages us to read the book aloud, not silently in the modern manner. This is something that I have done on occasions, not in the context of public worship, which only allows us to hear a few verses, but a whole narrative sequence (such as the story of Joseph) or a complete New Testament letter at one sitting. I too can testify, as does Michael, that in this way one hears and understands certain things for the first time. It is also a way of liberating ourselves from the superstition that there is only one meaning in a text, which this or that author has quarried once and for all. Theological exegesis expects there to be fresh insight to be gathered, and reads the text (or listens to it being read) with that expectation.

It would be a disservice to this work even to hint that it steps back into the past. The author has not merely used the resources of modern commentators on the Book of Esther, he is thoroughly modern in his engagement with, and insight into the contemporary struggle for faith. What emerges through the text is an honest, surprising and costly account of atonement, very different from the sedate and sometimes chilling versions, depicting transactions that scarcely touch the marrow of our doubts and failures.

Finally, a personal word. I was for nine years Michael's diocesan bishop. I conducted and preached at his institution, and in our case there was a genuine mutuality, which is the not always fulfilled potential of the pastoral relationship of bishop and parish priest. From our various contacts I treasure the memory of seeing a copy of a large commentary on Paul's letter to the Galatians on the family kitchen table. The sight was a surprise and delight in equal measure. Our church requires of its clergy a commitment to diligence in the study of the Holy Scriptures, even more emphatically of its bishops. There are no short cuts to the discipline of spending time and energy in this task. Balancing these against the inevitable demands of administration and pastoral work is no small skill. This book, however, is the outcome of a commitment which I deeply respect. I pray it may be an inspiration to many others to renew their vision of life-long learning in the service of Christ.

Stephen Sykes
31 May, 2002

Acknowledgements

I am grateful both to the congregation of St Paul's Church, Cambridge, and Bishop Stephen Sykes for the opportunity of a sabbatical in which to write up my sermon series on Esther.

I would particularly like to thank Diane Hicks for typing up the original manuscript, those who offered their insights on the original sermons and the first draft of the manuscript, and those who encouraged me to keep going with this, my first book.

I would also like to thank Diana Lipton for giving me the initial spark for my typological interpretation of the story of Esther via her unpublished paper in which she compares Xerxes to God.

Introduction

As the summer of 1997 drew to a close I was wondering what might occupy our collective thinking and experience in the coming months at St Paul's Church in Cambridge. As part of the body of those committed to the Bible as God's self-revelation, who seek to be open to engage with God, his word and our experience, what was to be our focus for the autumn?

One Sunday morning I sat in my office preparing for a service. The telephone rang. It was my mother, who said, 'I think you had better go indoors and look at the television if you haven't heard the news yet.' I did as she suggested. You will have already realized what I was to hear.

I am no royalist and, unlike my wife, I am not particularly interested in the activities of the Royal Family. More particularly, I am not concerned about their relationships, hopes, fears, loneliness or, indeed, wardrobes. Nevertheless, something touched me that morning and that week which seemed to affect many in this nation and across the globe similarly. The subject matter for our forthcoming reflections and a linked sermon series seemed to recommend itself. I needed to look no further than the book of Esther.

This small book of the Bible in some ways was an unlikely candidate for late twentieth-century study. It is set, whether its historicity is accepted or not, in the fifth century BC. At the time the known world was ruled by a despot of particular paternalistic, chauvinistic, violent and whimsical tendencies. Thus it is historically, geographically, socially and culturally far distant from the modern western world. It is a short story (which is always an advantage) of sexual politics, violence, vengeance, political intrigue and murder. Surprisingly, it makes no mention of God, prayer, worship or religion. Furthermore, it is one of only two books in the Bible (the other being Ruth) that make a woman the central figure.

As the events of the week following Diana's death came and went, the particular occasion for the series faded but the relevance of the story of Esther grew. The life and death of another remarkable twentieth-century woman, Mother Teresa, who died that same week, seemed less celebrated. This says something about our human and particularly our western predicament. Be that as it may, something was touched in many of us. There was a common denominator between these two very different women. They were prepared to follow in the way of the one, Jesus, who was also prepared to 'reach out and touch'. They brought comfort and hope to many, and in this sense they were like Esther. I was particularly struck by an account of a homeless person tackled by a journalist who wanted to know why he was so affected by the death of Diana, with whom he surely could have had nothing in common. The journalist argued that she was born into privilege, well fed, well groomed, well educated, never wanted for anything money could buy, had been married to a prince, adulated by millions, a friend to the great, famous and good. The homeless person apparently retorted, 'You don't have any idea of what it means to be homeless.'

What did the service at Westminster Abbey tell us of the spirituality of the nation? Powerful features were a procession extended by public demand, an accessible service involving a gay pop star accompanied by his partner, a eulogy on the complementary merits of duty and vulnerability, applause that rippled into the interior of the Abbey from the crowd outside, a spirituality perhaps encapsulated by the single word 'Mummy' on the coffin. It was my conviction that not only the spirituality of the book of Esther but its world view or metanarrative offered a far too long-hidden truth about reality and was particularly accessible to our nation at such a time as this. The hostility of Christian tradition – Martin Luther said, 'I am so hostile to it that I wish it did not exist', and Lewis B. Paton wrote in 1908, 'the book is so conspicuously lacking in religion it should never have been included in the Bible' – to the book of Esther seemed good reason to suspect that it might contain a spirituality and world view peculiarly relevant to the postmodern, secular twentieth-century west.

On Maundy Thursday evening in 1998, symbolically enough, a number of us celebrated an informal communion service together. The rain was pouring down and in quiet moments we could hear the deluge hitting the roof. 'It was like being in Noah's Ark,' someone said later.

The following day I learned that a friend and member of our congregation had been trying to get through to us on the telephone to tell us the story of his family's remarkable deliverance from what at one point he believed was going to be death. He had turned off the A1 due to traffic congestion and had driven through a couple of giant puddles before he realized that the third was no puddle but a lake – the result of a river having burst its banks. It was getting dark, it was freezing cold, and the rain was pouring down. As the water began to fill the car, his nine-year-old daughter, not surprisingly, became hysterical. He got everyone out and swam with her on his back to 'dry' land before going back for his wife, who by this time was seated on top of the car. He and his wife realized they were miles from anywhere, lost, cold, soaked to the skin, frightened and in a perilous situation. Just as he said to his wife, 'I think we had better pray,' a man driving a JCB arrived, pulled their car out of the water and took them to the nearest pub. They had been rescued from the record-breaking floods of Easter 1998.

I tell you this story to illustrate what I think the Bible means by salvation or deliverance. The above events can be interpreted, depending upon the 'faith' that one has, as follows:

1   God immediately answered their prayer and intervened out of compassion. In his power, he sent the man with the JCB to their rescue.

2 In their stars it was not their time to go, and therefore their
   death would have been impossible.
3 It was just 'one of those things', a coincidence, a timely reversal of fortune.
4 It was a combination of any or all of these possibilities.

Whatever it was, on Easter Sunday morning we celebrated their
remarkable (miraculous) deliverance as a church family.

The story of Esther is very definitely in the realms of options
two and three above. It presents a secular telling of a story of
deliverance. The majority of the Bible seems to me to be in the
realms of option one, a sacred telling of deliverance. However, I
believe that Jesus fulfils this sacred history in every respect in a
secular way, finally without any miraculous intervention. Furthermore, he stretches our understanding of deliverance beyond
breaking point. This can be demonstrated by retelling the story
of the family in the flood as follows:

> The man in the JCB arrived, attempted to rescue the family but died
> in the flood with them, in the early hours of Good Friday 1998. We
> met as a church family in shock and tears that Easter Sunday
> morning, only to be surprised beyond belief when the same JCB
> driver turned up, assured us that our friends had indeed been deliv-
> ered as we had hoped, though we would not be seeing them, and that
> we need not be afraid. He then disappeared.

This would have been a deliverance that for all the world looks
and feels like non-deliverance. It just so happens that this is the
Christian gospel. I have come to believe that God's presence is
experienced in his absence; life is experienced in death. We celebrate a sacrament of death both as we break bread and as we are
broken. Ultimately deliverance is a matter of trust because for
most of us, most of the time, neither the intervention of God nor
the luck, chance or coincidences of life deliver the outcome we
crave. Whether we choose to give up and walk away, get angry,
grow bitter, grit our teeth and plod on or live for today, I believe
he draws us all to himself through the gate of the final and

definitive tragedy – death. We shall wake from death to the ever-lasting day.

It was my prayer, hope and ambition for a very ordinary, failing, mixed and mixed-up congregation – as we are at St Paul's, just as every congregation is – that the story of Esther might enlighten, encourage and enable us along the way. I pray and hope that it will strengthen you too on your journey.

1

The Historical and Cultural Context

It is our task in this book to find the meaning of Esther and the purpose for which the book was written, as well as its particular Christology, so that our hearts may burn within us (Lk. 24:32) as we read of this strange 'star' set in the Old Testament firmament. The book of Esther takes up the themes of God's absence in a strange land, of God's non-intervention on behalf of his people and of God's seeming indifference to his covenant, and points us firmly towards Jesus. Among other themes to emerge will be exile, oppression, male domination and reversibility. In my first chapter I shall attempt to place Esther within her historical context and to expand upon the beginnings of the story in chapter 1 of the biblical book.

If you have not already done so, please read the whole of Esther to get the flavour of the book, the style of the writer and a feel for the content. It would also be helpful to read Ezra and Nehemiah.

These three biblical books complete the set of seventeen that record what I call the 'sacred historical thread'. The burden of their content is the deliverance of God's people, as representatives of all humankind, from slavery in a foreign land to freedom and blessing in the Promised Land, which has Jerusalem and the Temple at its heart. Unsurprisingly, this is also the burden of the seventeen prophetic books. Esther, however, stands out as not obviously being taken up with the focus of this sacred history – the Temple in Jerusalem. Indeed, the book apparently sets

its face against this history. How many of us have heard a
sermon on the subject of Esther? The book of Esther, then, is
something of an oddity in the selective biblical recording of
'world' history.

Let us turn to the Old Testament for a brief summary of its
biblical and historical content. The Babylonian King
Nebuchadnezzar had placed Judah under submission in around
606 BC, and thus began the seventy years of servitude prophesied
by Jeremiah (29:10). In 586 BC Nebuchadnezzar destroyed Jerusalem and exiled the Israelites to Babylon (Jer. 25:9–11). At the
end of this period in 536 BC many exiles returned under the edict
of Cyrus (recorded in Ezra 1). Cyrus had overcome Babylon and
established Persia in its place as ruler of the known world.
Further returns of exiles occurred under the enlightened rules of
Darius, recorded in Ezra, and of Artaxerxes, at which time the
walls of Jerusalem were rebuilt.

Perhaps nothing captures the feelings and mood of these
returning exiles better than Nehemiah 1:4–6:

> When I heard these things [that the walls of Jerusalem were broken
> down and its gates burned], I sat down and wept. For some days I
> mourned and fasted and prayed before the God of heaven. Then I
> said: 'Oh Lord, God of heaven, the great and awesome God, who
> keeps his covenant of love with those who love him and obey his
> commands, let your ear be attentive and your eyes open to hear the
> prayer your servant is praying before you day and night for your ser-
> vants, the people of Israel.'

To the Patriarchs, the Promised Land was the focus for the
renewal of the covenant in its royal form (2 Sam. 7). David, Jerusalem, the Son of David and the Temple are, in one form after
another, the central theme of the entire sacred history of the Old
Testament from Genesis 12 to the last recorded events of that
history in the book of Nehemiah nearly two millennia later. Out
of that sacred history and chronological sequence is plucked this
little book of Esther. It is placed at the end of that history,
and was to be followed by a further four-hundred years of silence

(cf. Gen. 50:26 – Ex. 1:8) before the revelation of the fulfilment of the promise of all sacred history – Jesus.

In this overarching biblical context, therefore, it seems to me that Esther is not merely to be enjoyed as an amusing story, but deserves at least as much Christological interpretation as any other portion of Scripture. Indeed, I believe that it possibly deserves more attention precisely because it is the 'last' historical book. It lays a foundation for our understanding of the work and presence of God in this world that needs to be held alongside the rest of the sacred history, and provides a significant window into the mind and heart of Jesus. Jesus takes up all the themes and types of the sacred history, but chooses finally to make them manifest not by powerful intervention but by powerless non-intervention. The Esther story provides us with a delightful fore-taste thereof. Ultimately the Cross, at the heart of the at-one-ment, was totally unexpected, unacceptable and unattractive, and still is – precisely because Jesus allowed it to happen and refused to come down, and only thus demonstrated his authority and the promised deliverance.

This Son of David, prince of peace, Temple destroyer, Temple builder, the one and only seed, is the only faithful remnant. All others have failed. He will ultimately refuse to make visible the mighty deliverance he has accomplished and leave this world pretty much as he found it. He will also ultimately refuse to demonstrate the fulfilment of the promise of the kingdom, and of life, by works of power, and will remain on the Cross only to return briefly to reassert the promise and its fulfilment. He will then depart so that we might 'experience' his presence in his absence through a sacrament of death, and not resurrection.

How are such exiles, failures and wilderness dwellers – away from the land of promise and blessing – to live? Let us return to Esther, and the feelings of the Jews. In the sense of their non-return 'home', these people are at best second class and at worst failures and outcasts to their inheritance. Are they indeed cast off, without hope, no longer God's people, no longer covenant beneficiaries, under God's curse and not his blessing? Will this be the writer's conclusion? From the perspective of sacred history, this must be the case. It certainly seems to have been the orthodox Judaean view *vis-à-vis* the Samaritans (who were assimilated Jewish non-returnees) at the time of Jesus. However, strangely, at the same time there was a very strong monotheistic tradition among the exiled people of the synagogue and the book who regularly went on pilgrimage back to Jerusalem at festival time. These people had maintained faith and hope and their own understanding of covenant inclusion, despite not being part of the returning remnant.

It is worth noting in passing that both James and Peter address their letters specifically to this group: 'the twelve tribes scattered among the nations' (Jas. 1:1) and 'God's elect, strangers [scattered] in the world' (1 Pet. 1:1). Does God's covenant to the Twelve Tribes stand despite the fact that they have not returned to Jerusalem, and indeed have deliberately chosen not to live there? It would seem that the answer is a resounding 'yes'. In fact, God's covenant with the Twelve Tribes is certainly not based on their faithfulness, and indeed stands in and with their unfaithfulness. This will be revealed powerfully by God's faithfulness in and through Jesus, the 'man who looks intently into the perfect law that gives freedom ... [and who is] blessed in what he does' (Jas. 1:25), the 'only one Lawgiver and Judge' (Jas. 4:12). Even these people find that they are 'a chosen people, a royal priesthood, a holy nation, a people belonging to God ... Once you were not a people, but now you are the people of God; once you had not received mercy, but now you have received mercy' (1 Pet. 2:9–10). These people are no longer 'not a people' (Lo-Ammi), no longer 'not loved' (Lo-Ruhamah) and no longer 'unforgiven' (Jezreel) (Hos. 1:1 – 2:1). The covenant cursing of Hosea's three children of harlotry has indeed been reversed. The rejected stone that causes stumbling (1 Pet. 2:8) is also the cornerstone of the Temple (1 Pet. 2:6) in Jesus.

If such as these are forgiven, accepted, loved and restored, despite their greater knowledge of the covenant and therefore culpability, how much more will those ostensibly outside the covenant of God – the Gentiles – be given similar cause to celebrate as we too find ourselves restored, embraced, included and made alive with Christ (1 Pet. 3:18 – 4:6) under the umbrella (rainbow) of the covenant made with all humankind by God in the days of Noah?

Now, the above may have seemed a long and heavy theological introduction to an amusing tale of political intrigue and sexual power play. I make no apologies. This story must be read in the setting intended by those who put the canon of Scripture together, as overseen by the Holy Spirit, if its fullest and richest seams are to be mined. So, now back to Esther chapter 1: the tale of two particular non-returnees from the land of exile, and their compatriots, living in a foreign land under the rule of a less-than-enlightened despot, King Xerxes of Persia.

Please read chapter 1, preferably aloud for best effect and impact. I do not propose to undertake a detailed study of each verse. There are two particular works that I would recommend wholeheartedly for such help: Jon D. Levenson's *Esther* (London: SCM Press, 1997) and Michael V. Fox, *Character and Ideology in the Book of Esther* (Columbia, SC: University of South Carolina Press, 1991). I will, when I feel it appropriate, stop and look at a verse or word in greater detail, but generally I will try to maintain both the sense of the story and its plot, as well as its Christological portent.

Chapter 1 of the book of Esther sets the entirely secular scene. What a Jewish response might be, we will find out in chapter 2. Suffice it to say, for now, it is not the response of Nehemiah, nor indeed of Daniel (Dan.1:8; 6:10), in which the more narrowly defined covenantal 'separatism' is in stark contrast to the 'accommodation' we will find in our story.

Let us look again at the narrative to gain the flavour of the genre or style of the storytelling. The story unravels as follows. King Xerxes, ruler of 127 provinces, whose beneficence has extended to all his peoples in a banquet lasting for six months, follows this up with a seven-day banquet for all the inhabitants of the capital city, from the least to the greatest. This king is lord of all the earth, has power over all, and his grace and favour extend to all. By the end of the chapter he has, under advice from his closest legal advisors (the highest and wisest in the land

[1:13–14]), promulgated a royal decree that 'every man should be ruler over his own household' (1:22).

The events give us pause for thought. Why draw more attention to the king's own inability to rule over his own wife, Queen Vashti, and therefore his household? Queen Vashti had refused (1:12) to obey the royal command and appear before the king: for punishment, ironically, she was banished from the royal presence. Moreover, once Xerxes' drunkenness (1:10) has passed, and likewise the anger (2:1) that issued from his vain pride, he realizes that he has cut off his nose to spite his face – he seems to miss her (2:1).

Do the men of the kingdom really need the royal decree to go on maintaining the status quo of patriarchy? With whom are our sympathies by the end of the chapter if not Queen Vashti, called upon to display herself to a drunken party of men? And what of the king's council? 'Queen Vashti has done wrong, not only against the king but also against all the nobles and the peoples of all the provinces of King Xerxes' (1:16). Thus says the narrator, but what have we really learned?

The picture the writer gives us of this absolute ruler of all the earth is of a vain fool; a weak, indecisive despot with absolute power. In such a kingdom under such governance any minority group, whether social or sexual, is endangered. Such rule will not be equitable but unpredictable. It will not be based upon the good of all, and certainly not organized for the weakest and the marginalized, but rather for, by and on behalf of the self-interested, the self-seeking and powerful. Powerful men will be very keen to affirm and maintain the status quo, not for the king's benefit nor for that of the people, but for their own ends. With such a weak, mindless fool on the throne, let the reader take note, the lower levels of society must beware.

It is my conviction that the writer intends us to laugh and enjoy the joke at the king's expense – the story is a comedy. It is also, however, a tragedy over which our writer intends us to weep. The writer also want us to draw the parallel, by contrast, with the one who is not merely lord of all the earth, but Lord of heaven as well; who is not merely lord of this small cameo of universal history, but Lord of all history; and whose rule of law is not capricious or malevolent, but is based on justice and equity. In addition, they wish us to pick out the attributes of Yahweh by contrasting him with King Xerxes. Yahweh is Elohim, as the writer of Daniel (4:1–3; 4:34–35; 6:26–27) makes explicit. Xerxes represents God in our story. (My thanks to Diana Lipton, whose unpublished paper on the woman's lot in Esther led me to this conclusion.)

The writer is deliberately opening up questions for the reader that reflect real issues for exiles living in a strange land. These are real issues for the members of any minority group (racial, social or sexual) living in a hierarchical, patriarchal society (the 'lot' of slave, Gentile and female referred to in Galatians 3:28 perhaps not unsurprisingly springs to mind). They are:

1 How do I live in such a perilous culture?
2 Can I expect deliverance in such a culture and, if so, what form might this take?
3 Is the rule of law the last word?

I believe that the writer is also setting down a key marker for the story that will unfold when they tell us that the royal decree – however ridiculous, vainly motivated and unnecessary – is none the less irreversible (1:19).

It is my view that the whole book of Esther is structured around this issue of reversibility. Deliverance is manifest as the powerless are empowered, as the last are made first, and the least greatest. Reversibility is particularly and peculiarly demonstrated in our story as an ethnic minority represented by a woman is elevated to first in the land.

Esther is the type of Jesus. She depicts the deliverer who brings about the reversal of circumstances for those on the underside, who brings them justice and equity, and who elevates them over those who would bring them nothing but dishonour. I am convinced that Esther represents a female Christ figure. This has huge implications, not only for any debate about female priesthood, but far more importantly for the role, place, value, equality and status of women in God's universal, restored kingdom.

I believe that our writer wishes us to see the banquet for the least and the greatest (1:5) as an archetype for the kingdom of heaven. The event is comprehensive and has the most extravagant nature (1:6–8), and includes all people throughout the world at the table of the king. Without wishing to state the obvious, a certain sacred parallel and conclusion to world history springs to mind, as does a certain other 'story' on the lips of the Lord Jesus. Furthermore, Jesus' penchant for describing the kingdom in such extravagant, joyful party scenes – to say nothing of his habit of being found at table with 'sinners' throughout the gospels – suggests that despite the secular, Gentile, foreign dress of this first chapter of Esther, we are none the less not far from the kingdom of God.

As this may be too fanciful for the taste of some, let us revert to the story itself and in particular the significance of the number seven in the narrative. The lord of all the earth – Xerxes – hosts a second banquet that lasts seven days (1:5). On the seventh day, Xerxes commands the seven eunuchs (1:10), and takes counsel (1:14) from his seven nobles. Note also that Esther is assigned seven maids (2:9) and is taken to Xerxes in the seventh year of his reign (2:16). All this makes me suspect that our writer, whom I believe has a plan in writing the book, makes these references to the number seven with a purpose in mind. The number seven is not only biblical shorthand for completeness – notably in Genesis 1 and Revelation 1:20 – but also, because of its use at the beginning and end of the biblical account of world history (not to mention the weekly cycle of our lives), denotes the oneness of all creation, history and peoples. The use of the number seven in this context, therefore, serves to underscore the picture of the lord of all the earth with all the peoples of the earth at his table. The writer is painting a universal, archetypal picture of world-embracing scope wherein both by direct parallel and by direct contrast they show us the kingdom of heaven – if we will only have eyes to see.

We cannot leave the chapter without reflecting on the parallel universe of the women under Queen Vashti, their representative at the table (1:9). The writer will offer us in later chapters a very pragmatic wisdom in the person and work of Esther. In such a society as this the stance of Queen Vashti, by contrast, is futile. However much we may empathize and side with Queen Vashti, in such a culture and context a more compliant, subtle approach is necessary. This will not suit the defiant revolutionary spirit in our midst, since it calls for compromises in behaviour, actions and attitudes. In an ideal world we might not wish for such realism, but our writer's tale – despite its genre, and perhaps the more so because of it – is ruthlessly realistic about the role, place and opportunities of those on the underside of society. Tragically, throughout history and in too many cultures, this situation has been repeated in the oppression of ethnic minorities and particularly of women. Nor is the way in which that same underclass might realize in any meaningful way the reversal of their lot – deliverance – any more realizable. The writer of Esther, from their first-hand experience, enables us to feel the full weight of male oppression of women through the telling of Esther's story.

Domination, rule and obedience, which were never the intention of the Creator but rather the curse of the Fall (Gen. 3), will certainly no longer have any place in God's restored kingdom. The submission (see Phil. 2:5) of Christ who, like Esther before him, demonstrated this behavioural pattern in the world for the sake of others (Mk. 10:45), should characterize all our relationships until then (Eph. 5:21). On the last day the fullness of our deliverance will be completely manifest when all will be equally honoured, valued, accepted and loved. No one will be required to live in fear any longer, in a parallel, shadowy world to that of the rich, great, powerful and famous. On that last great day the least and the great (1:5) will indeed be seated together at the king's son's banquet (Mt. 22:1–14).

2

The King's Palace

To begin with, read chapter 2 of Esther again. If it is not too embarrassing, do this out loud. I repeat that I am convinced that such a process adds something to the usual quiet internal reading process.

I have just taken my own advice. Immediately a number of things have jumped out at me, as I hope and trust they did for you. We have a massive cultural gap to bridge and our own individual response to be aware of. This chapter is about the comings and goings of the king's harem. This may be surprising biblical material in the view of some. They may think it could have been made more acceptable if the writer had at least pronounced some moral judgements. Instead, the whole story turns on Esther's acquiescence and submission to the beautifying process within the harem, with its inevitable and logical conclusion – her 'turn' (2:12,15) in the king's bed. Chapter 2 also introduces Esther's guardian, Mordecai.

The Bible is full of thoroughly earthy, human, ordinary experience. If it were not, then the biblical revelation of God would be reduced or elevated to some unrealistic transcendent, mystical, measly, spiritual level. The Bible's view of God cannot be reduced or elevated in this way by either the biblical critic or the would-be heavenly minded. What we read in the Bible shows us that God will not allow himself to be removed from the real world. Of course we are entirely free to do what we want with what we learn about him. If we are to treat him with integrity, we will not be able to cast the God we find in the Bible in our own image.

If we have a real need to breathe the air of morality and judgement, we do not have far to look. The Bible contains God's outline for responsible and responsive human living in the Ten Commandments. It also contains his judgement upon our culpability and failure to live so – the prophets' writings are full of devastating and utterly justified analyses of injustice and the abuse of power by both individual and nation under the umbrella of God's covenant: 'If you fully obey the Lord your God and carefully follow all his commands ... you will be blessed' (Deut. 28:1–3) ... 'However, if you do not obey ... you will be cursed' (Deut. 28:15–16).

If, however, we long for the fresher air of forgiveness and mercy, fully conscious that 'but for the grace of God there go I', then perhaps we need to hear God's final verdict on a disobedient, covenant-breaking humankind. It is to be found on the lips of Jesus at the supreme moment of revelation, as he hung on the Cross: 'Father forgive them ...' (Lk. 23:34). The God who reveals himself in the Bible I read is thoroughly transcendent and heavenly, but at the same time totally earthy, involved and realistic about the world, humankind and his involvement in it. He is just, fair and pure, and in his working knowledge of us in our relationships with one another and with him he is unconditionally accepting, loving and forgiving. God, it seems to me, in the biblical form of his self-revelation, and indeed in all other forms, refuses to allow himself to be reduced or pigeon-holed (for his claim to this kind of divinity, read Mk. 11 – 15).

Let us return to the world presented to us by our author. From this chapter and its record of a particular event in a particular place at a particular time, we gain a view of the way women are being treated by men. It appears to me that our author, if they have a judgement about this, does not make it explicit in this chapter, or indeed in the book. We are only able to see the world from our author's perspective by implication. The message is no less powerful for that. It seems to me that one purpose – if not the main purpose of this little story – is to communicate how people were to live in that society. It was a society that was unfair, where power was abused. (Of course, if we happen to identify with the powerful men in the story and their abuse of power in relation to women and ethnic minorities, we shall view it differently.) God appears to have been absent or powerless, or at least permitted the status quo and injustice to persist. When we look at our own cultural clothes, what do we find? In the world in which we live there is injustice, abuse of power and lack of intervention of God. That is why I sense that this book may have something particular and special to communicate to us today.

The more discerning reader may have noted the author's failure to make any moral judgement about the injustice of the male–female relationships in the story so far (and any comment about monogamous marriage). The author underlines the dilemma that we as supposedly more enlightened modern readers may be feeling by contrasting the understandable disobedience of Queen Vashti (1:12) with the compliance and obedience (2:13) of Esther (2:17). Queen Vashti refuses to be displayed as a sex object at the king's banquet. Esther passively accepts her fate. She is taken to the king's palace (2:8), is given twelve months' beauty treatment (2:12) and finally taken to the king as a chattel at his sexual disposal (2:15).

Our author seems to have set a demanding agenda. If, as I believe, the story is concerned with male–female sexual politics and the issue of gender justice, they have carefully and deliberately emphasized aspects of events that we as readers feel call for some kind of 'resolution'. The story, as it unfolds, will relieve some of the tension, but if it is a Hollywood ending we are after we shall be disappointed. There will be a remarkable turnaround in the fortunes of Esther and her race at this particular point in their shared history, but the structure of society will not have changed one bit. After that time there will be many further sociological and historical examples of sexual abuse, injustice and what we now know as ethnic cleansing. The intervention of the Christ who will put all things right will, equally paradoxically, leave the world apparently very much as he found it. People will continue to indulge in sexual, racial and political abuse; processes that were endemic then, and despite the many modern advances in human rights, still continue all round the globe.

Rather than paint an ideal or indulge in sentimentalism, the author deliberately chooses to tell a shockingly realistic story. That is not to say that dreams or sentiment are inherently harmful. We just have to think of the pictures Jesus painted in his parables, or of Martin Luther King's 'I have a dream' speech, to realize the hold that an imaginative story or symbol can have. But in answer to the question 'How shall I live in the real world?' our author will not allow us to be self-indulgent or escapist. Whether we like it or not, this world, they confirm, is determined to oppress and abuse its most vulnerable and powerless members.

In the face of such realism we are left with the question of how we are to live, for we cannot escape. One answer is: enjoy a good story, dream a little, trust to luck but keep your eyes open, use your brain, be prepared to bite the bullet. For the sake of a higher principle and a greater good, be prepared to sacrifice some lower principles and some lesser goods, not to mention some down-right bads. I am not about to make a case for a particular hierarchy of principles. I'm sure we would all disagree about that. If you already feel drawn, or even compelled, to identify with Queen Vashti, I probably agree with you deep down. I am fundamentally a revolutionary, Protestant idealist – or at least I like to think I am. However, face me with the choice of complying and living or refusing and being banished – or worse, being executed – and I might change my hierarchy of principles. To side with Vashti at this point is to deny the need to read any more of Esther and to read any more of this book. The book of Esther, and my writing upon it, focuses on the consequence of Esther's pragmatic, self-demeaning compliance and of the king's demands and abuse of his power and position.

At this point, let us consider briefly a further contrast that the Bible itself offers us: that between Daniel and his friends and Esther. This contrast is even more evident in the Hebrew Scriptures, where the books of Daniel and Esther are found together. Daniel and his friends refuse the king's food (Dan. 1:8) and decide to protest against the royal decrees of Nebuchadnezzar (Dan. 3:12) and Darius (Dan. 6:10). In this way they confront

two absolute rulers, with the result that their God, Yahweh, is
honoured over and against all the gods of the nations as the Lord
of heaven and earth because of his miraculous intervention (Dan.
1:15; 3:28–29; 6:21–22,26,27).

In these two books we have two very similar contexts and two
radically differing responses. Two very different hierarchies of
principles are applied by the two heroes. It may be argued that
sexuality is less important than worship of and prayer to God, so
the former might legitimately be sacrificed to the latter. Con-
versely, I feel that our sexuality is a major part of our having been
made in the image of God, and that worship and prayer would be
seriously compromised by such a hierarchy. Be that as it may, but
surely no one would argue that one's dietary preference (Dan. 1)
is a higher principle than sexuality. The two writers of Esther and
Daniel are pointing up for us a striking contrast: a difference in
world view. Daniel and his friends represent the 'religious', who
may expect the intervention of God on their behalf (as happens
in their 'miraculous' deliverance from both furnace and lions).
Esther represents the 'irreligious', who have no particular expectation of intervention by God for their deliverance. Note that this
is not the same thing as saying that it is only the religious who
experience God's miraculous intervention, or that the irreligious
do not. That would quite clearly be untrue.

The paradox of our author's world view is, of course, as
follows:

1 Despite the lack of miraculous intervention deliverance
   occurs anyway.
2 Whether God intervenes miraculously or not, and whether
   deliverance is experienced or not, the faithful will against all
   reason trust God anyway (4:14, cf. Dan. 3:18).
3 God chooses to reveal his providential deliverance through
   coincidence and so-called luck rather than through some
   mighty miracle.

The author of Esther is offering us an alternative and equally biblical world view. Although it is included in the Bible, it is largely

ignored by commentators and Christian readers alike. This is presumably in line with the principle of a canon within a canon: that is, we read the bits we like and that fit our theological or devotional framework and conveniently ignore those that do not. I believe that the alternative world view found in the story of Esther is peculiarly relevant to our postmodern western culture. In its non-religious – indeed irreligious – language, viewpoint and form it is particularly accessible to us. At the same time, and quite unexpectedly, its outcome also conforms to the more 'normal', 'sacred', biblical view of God as active in history for the deliverance of his people and of all humankind. It is merely the means that differ. In Esther we see 'providence' over and against, in tandem with or parallel to miraculous intervention.

Ultimately I am suggesting that there is a metanarrative or storyline for all history and that this has one theme – deliverance. This deliverance is experienced in a reversal of circumstances, whatever the language used. In a narrative this deliverance may be attributed to God directly through his intervention, perhaps in the form of a miracle. Alternatively it may not be attributed to him directly; his involvement may be implied by the way things turn around and turn out. Whichever happens, all will be well. It is deliverance that is at the heart of what we call reality. Our experience of that reality and that deliverance in some mysterious way is not only despite our circumstances, but because of them; it comes about not only from our suffering, fear, anxiety and loneliness but through them. Ultimately our experience of deliverance will not only be in and through death, but on the other side of it.

Now, after that long and heavy theological trawl, back to the story. We are in the company of a girl on the journey to becoming a woman in a patriarchal society where she is merely a pawn. Before looking at Esther's response to her circumstances and the consequences recorded for us in chapter 2, we need to look briefly at Mordecai, to whom we are introduced at this point, and at Esther's relationship with him.

I must admit to a certain resistance to and dislike of Mordecai. This is not merely because most commentators, it seems to me, wish to make him the hero of the book (which is itself sad and predictable, as he is male) but also because, on the evidence of the book itself, his motivation, character and conduct are so mixed. For example:

- He requires Esther to keep her ethnicity a secret (2:10) when his own Jewishness is both public and provocative (3:4).
- He refuses to comply (3:2 [like Vashti, 1:12]) with the king's command, yet expects Esther to do so (2:8).
- His male guardianship confines Esther to the king's harem (2:8).
- His ethnic pride puts Esther and the lives of all the Jews in jeopardy (3:9; 4:11).
- He is consequently repentant (4:1), but no less guilty of unnecessary and futile provocation (5:9).

To my mind, there is no doubt that Esther's pragmatic obedience and compliance is presented to us by the writer as the way to live in her world. This way is set in contrast to the futile and life-threatening disobedience of Vashti and Mordecai. In Mordecai's favour, it can be said that:

- In making the plot against the king known (2:19–23) he acts with loyalty and courage (of course, he – like Haman, his secular counterpart and adversary to be introduced in chapter 3 – could also be accused of vain, naked ambition).
- In keeping Esther's ethnicity a secret he may not have been motivated by self-advancement or fear for himself (cf. Abraham in Genesis) but fear for what would happen to Esther if her ethnicity were discovered or if she were disobedient to the king.
- In requiring Esther to submit to the king he may have thought that to enter the king's harem was not a manifestation of the abuse of power for sexual gratification but, in the culture of the day, a much sought-after personal preferment. Certainly the quality of Esther's life would be assured in the harem.

I think on balance, however, that the writer reveals their hand and their underlying negativity towards the person of Mordecai in the story by their conscious attempt to draw comparison between Mordecai and King Saul in the genealogy (2:5; cf. 1 Sam. 9:1) (see J.D. Levenson, p. 56). This view, I believe, is confirmed when Haman is introduced to us as an Agagite (3:1), a reference to Agag, the ancient enemy of King Saul (1 Sam. 15). This suggests to me a significant typological interpretation alongside the more obvious personal, psychological and sociological explanation for the suspicion, hatred and dislike between the two men. Mordecai is successful over and against Haman; his ancestor Saul was not successful against Agag. There is also an unlikely reversal, with Haman becoming the unsuspecting agent of Mordecai's elevation (the opposite of the situation for his ancestor King Saul, for whom Agag served as the agent of dethronement). Even so, I believe – with all respect to Levenson – that it is Esther who, in becoming queen, is the successful typological fulfilment of the failure of King Saul. It is not Mordecai, who becomes Prime Minister. It seems to me that Esther is being presented as a type of David, the great servant king and covenant partner to Yahweh (2 Sam. 7).

It is Esther and not Mordecai who is presented in our story both as a type of prophet–priest mediator between Xerxes and his people (the parallel being God and humankind) and as a type of servant king set over and against the failed kingship of Saul. I believe she is additionally a fulfilment of the charismatic, spirit-filled 'elected' leadership through whom God delivered his people in the time of the Judges. It is Esther to whom the greater honour accrues. As we look to the fulfilment of this story in the person of Jesus, we are presented with a very particular view of kingship through the window of the person, work and submission of Queen Esther. From the author of this story I would say we have a very significant contribution to our understanding of the nature of kingship as fulfilled in Jesus. The failure of the mighty King Saul is partially fulfilled in the submission of the powerless, female Queen Esther, and points in a very distinctive way towards Jesus.

My understanding of the writer's perspective may or may not accord with your interpretation of the story. I am convinced, however, that our author is presenting an alternative, equally biblical, conclusion to that of other writers of the sacred record. The strange placing of Esther, out of chronological sequence, at the end of that sacred record of Old Testament history with its particular world view and its particular understanding of kingship, seems to me not merely to confirm this, but also to suggest a progression in biblical revelation or a hierarchy in world view, or perhaps both.

Thus armed, we may return to the person of Esther, who is consistently portrayed in non-religious terms. For instance, in her circumstances, might we not have expected her to have resorted to prayer? She might pray to plead that her fate might be avoided completely or, lacking that answer, that she might have the wisdom to know how and how not to behave. If that is our expectation, we are disappointed in this chapter (unless we wish to resort to the apocryphal additions) and we shall be perhaps more significantly disappointed as the story unfolds and the dangers increase in later chapters. There is no resort to the inner room of private prayer (cf. Dan. 6:10), nor is there resort to open and public praise of God after the deliverance (cf. Dan. 6:22,26,27).

I suggest that we are presented with two alternative views of the manner and means of God's accomplishment of his purpose to deliver his people. It is important to note the significant differences in response to such similar circumstances of God's agents of this deliverance, Daniel and Esther. It is also important to recognize that both are true, both are possible, both are good responses. While I am suggesting there may ultimately be a hierarchy, it is not the case that one is always or necessarily better than the other. Daniel's response might typically be described as 'separatist'; it emphasizes religious, cultural and ethnic identity and difference. Esther's response is describable as 'accommodationist'; it emphasizes our common identity with all people. Which emphasis seems preferable and most appropriate in particular circumstances will depend on personal temperament and on the situation. However, I would say that the separation of the people of God is not for their own sake but is intended as a sign to the world that God chooses to reveal his love of all humankind through a particular people. The moment that the people of God lose sight of this, then their separation for the sake of the world has become *separatism*, religious and futile.

I am suggesting that these two world views are based on the one grand metanarrative of the deliverance of all peoples by God. One view emphasises the unique role of God's covenant people; the other God's covenant with all humankind. One emphasizes the miracle of deliverance; the other the 'miracle' of coincidence. One emphasizes the power of the Almighty in accomplishing his sovereign purpose; the other demonstrates the fulfilment of that purpose through the operation of the free will of his enemies. One emphasizes the intervention of God; the other the throw of the die (3:7), coincidence – 'on this day' (9:1) – and luck – 'that night' (6:1). In the face of apparent impossibility of reversal of fate, let alone the irreversibility of God's (or Xerxes') own law, both world views emphasize impossible reversal made possible (Mt. 19:25–26), one in and through men (prophet, priest and king) and the other through a woman, Esther. Both world views are true. Both are fulfilled in Jesus, who is both king of kings and the servant of all; who is always in control yet who is able to fulfil his Father's purpose by putting himself at the mercy of his enemies; who in accomplishing our deliverance through his mighty resurrection does so only after his rejection, failure and death.

Esther, like Joseph before her (Gen. 39:4) finds favour with all those with whom she has contact (2:9,15) and ultimately with King Xerxes (2:17). We will have occasion later to look more closely at what I believe is the author's deliberate comparison of our heroine with such great biblical heroes of the faith. Let us for now merely state this comparison for the record. These men give us different aspects of the complete picture of deliverance fulfilled in Jesus (Lk. 2:52), as does Esther, who grows up full of wisdom, and as a model of submission who finds favour with everyone (2:15).

In conclusion, I want to highlight further our author's alternative view of biblical history that they will make almost explicit in 4:14. We have seen that their view is not unfolded in predictable covenantal terms such as 'If you do this ... then this will follow.' (This covenantal view accords to the more normative framework of the wisdom writers collected in the book of Proverbs.) Our writer believes and expresses, through a secular view of the world and its history, that it is through injustice, the unexpected and the reversal of fortunes – which are all too often our experience – that the fulfilment of that same covenant is experienced. (This less normative, more disordered view accords to that of the writers of the wisdom literature who speculated upon a reality that did not accord with that of the covenant, and indeed was often the very opposite, for example, you could not be cursed if you were righteous [Job] and you could not be blessed in this life if you were vain [Ecclesiastes].)

Our writer also takes seriously, rather than treating dismissively, what might be termed an astrological world view. The lot falls, the die is thrown (3:7), 'what will be will be'. We are the pawns, or possibly even some of the more important pieces: king, queen, bishop, knight or rook. Identify yourself in the story and with the characters as the cap best fits. The story of Esther can be seen as a game, the result of which, some would say, has already been decided. But has it?

The author makes the situation far worse for themselves and us by placing the casting of the die in the iron fist of a law that cannot be reversed and must be fulfilled to the letter (1:19). With modern-day astrologers there seems to be a greater variety of possible outcomes.

Now, it seems to me that this is one of our author's greatest accomplishments. If God is all-powerful and determined to accomplish his purpose, he can and will. If he is determined, however, at the same time to elicit a free reciprocal response of gratitude and love then it is imperative that in some mysterious, invisible, non-directive non-activity he allows us – humankind, his intended covenant, partners and lovers – complete freedom of choice. In a world where there is structural injustice within the rule of law and a desperate fatalism about the likely outcome, and sometimes seemingly a conspiracy between the two to thwart the purpose of deliverance and relationship, it seems to me that it is truly remarkable that such a purpose is accomplished without recourse to direct intervention. This truly is at-one-ment.

The writer unfolds their story and points us to a laying down of power on the part of the Almighty, despite his ability and desire to intervene and the desperate circumstances of Esther. The author demonstrates the lengths to which God is prepared to go in allowing us the freedom, however fatalistically and legalistically we may choose to use it, to go our own way. And yet God still ensures that the outcome of the game will be that we are found by him and receive his favour.

If we – whether powerful, imperialistic dominators and abusers or powerless, abused minorities – are not to confine one another to the drainpipe of an utterly predictable and inevitable fate, then God alone, without infringing our freedom to choose such a fate and without breaking the law of cause and effect, must accomplish the impossible reversal of fortune: that is, our deliverance. This is precisely what this story assures us he has done in Esther, who is a type of Christ. Even then, indeed even now, he waits patiently for our response. Those readers who desire the everlasting rule of equity and peace to be ushered in will be disappointed in Esther, and indeed in the Lord Jesus. That reign, that peace, that equity are for now only glimpsed. Yet we live by faith in the sure and certain hope that despite appearances, our deliverance, which has already been accomplished, is ours by that same faith and may be celebrated even now.

Cynical commentators speculate on the likelihood of a slave girl becoming queen in an alien land and being the agent of reversal for her people through a complicity and submission to the rule of law and patriarchy that brought about the fate of her people in the first place. They are right to speculate. Such eventualities are ridiculous, but it is in their very unlikeliness and unexpectedness, and in the repetition of the pattern (as in Joseph and Moses), that we may receive the assurance, through the eyes of faith, that ultimately all will be well. Sometimes, in our own experience, all will be well even before then. It isn't that our cup only and always runs over unexpectedly, but that far more consistently and persistently our cup is poured out. We may see both situations, through the eyes of faith, as places in which we find the Lord's blessing.

3

The Plot Emerges

Now read chapter 3 of Esther. I have just done this myself and, as I often find on a Sunday when I hear the Bible read out loud, I find it hard to resist standing up immediately and getting into action. The material seems pregnant; crying out for expression.

Let us begin then. Is there anything that strikes you particularly? It is worth making a note of those passages, verses or words that draw your attention, and then thinking about why. Such a process, whatever the wider biblical, theological interpretation of the passage concerned, has particular personal significance for you. It is indeed the word of God to you, and yet it is delightfully and inevitably very different from what I receive. I remember one Sunday morning a visitor thanking me warmly for the sermon, which was certainly an encouragement, but I realized that what had been the word of God for him that morning was not only a complete misunderstanding of what I had been trying to say, but was also in my view a complete misapplication of the text. Such are the ways of the mysterious, invisible activity of the word made flesh, manifested in our midst through the operation of the Holy Spirit. Indeed, if this were not the case I'm not sure I would dare to preach such a word week by week or to write these comments. In the end I'm not responsible for the truth: he, Jesus, will authenticate himself to us all, whether my attempts at elucidation are successful or not. This is a relief to me as I write and I hope to you as you read. Relax, enjoy the tale, take it – and my recasting of it – as you will, in the sure knowledge that whether our understanding is 'right' or not, we shall be found by him.

One of the lessons of this ridiculously improbable, historical–comic tragedy is that we must lighten up, 'get a life' and enjoy it. We are meant to enjoy it – the story and, indeed, our lives as well – whether in patient trust as circumstances turn downwards, or in robust thanksgiving as they turn upwards again. Some simple, practical words of Jesus spring to mind. He said, 'do not worry about your life ... do not worry about tomorrow' (Mt. 6:25,34), but trust your heavenly father whose provision of bread may be seen as both material and sacramental. Jesus' brother James said, 'Consider it pure joy, my brothers, whenever you face trials ... because you know that the testing of your faith develops perseverance' (Jas. 1:2–3). The same message is given in Psalms 1 and 15.

You may feel I have a tendency to digress. Let me try to begin again. Verse 1 may strike you as strange. 'After these events' presumably means those events of chapters 1 and 2, in which Queen Vashti is deposed and her replacement sought and found in the virgin Esther, and more particularly those of 2:19–23, where Mordecai saves King Xerxes' life. In verse 1, however, we learn that 'Xerxes honoured Haman' instead. Note the injustice of Mordecai's loyalty and service not being rewarded, while his enemy – as Haman turns out to be – is elevated in his place. The writer's purpose is to turn up the heat and increase the tension. Events move rapidly now and time is concertinaed in this middle section (chapters 3 – 8) of the book. In chapter 3 events overtake the Jews and we will be left deliberately in a state of anxiety and tension. Will the Jews be delivered? If so, how, and by whom?

In my second chapter I briefly outlined the possible ways in which Mordecai's motivation and character can be viewed in the light of his requirements that Esther should keep her ethnicity a secret and comply with the king's decree. However, here we find Mordecai himself refusing to comply (3:2) on the grounds of his ethnicity (3:4). 'Hypocrite' is the word that springs to my mind, for the writer does not give us the more positive separatist interpretation of Mordecai's behaviour, unlike the writer of Daniel.

In my view, the writer does not want us to hold Mordecai up as a hero because he refused to surrender his male pride and bow to Haman, who is merely the Prime Minister. After all, in the previous chapter, Esther, at Mordecai's behest, was required to surrender her body (let alone her ethnic identity) to the whim and fancy of the king himself. Instead what is revealed is, I believe, male caprice and, ironically, this is the very reason for the unfolding of the story as we have it recorded. We may wish to regard Mordecai's provocation of Haman as the 'happy fault' as a result of which all Jews experienced deliverance. I think we would be wise not to give him the credit, just as in our own response to 'grace abounding' we ought not to attribute credit to ourselves – and particularly not when we are at fault. It is true, of course, that it is precisely because we recognize our own faults that we are more amazed at our reversal of fortune, more contrite about our folly and sin and more grateful to almighty God. It occurs to me that I have already presumed upon both the universality of sin and your agreement with me about its existence, and indeed upon your personal participation in it. I will presume upon this further as my analysis proceeds. My interpretation of Esther is largely based on the presumption of universality as well as on the ability of an individual not merely to symbolize a race – or, as we shall see, all humankind – but also to represent them typologically. All are one and one is all.

This needs some explanation. I will try to explain my understanding of how a person, thing or institution can be a type of Jesus later in this chapter. In summary, I don't simply mean that we can be enabled to see or grasp better the significance of his person and work. I also mean that we can actually participate in him and he in us now, just as those types and those whom they affected participated in him then. Jesus really is the same yesterday, today and forever (Heb. 13:8).

I suppose I feel it is self-evident that the greed, self-seeking, selfishness, lust, hate, anger and other emotions that I experience, and that I observe in others, are universal, and that I do not need to make a case for their universality. This doesn't mean we are all as bad as each other. We are all a mixture of both good and bad, some at one end of the spectrum and some at the other. But it does seem to me to be self-evident that we are all part of that spectrum. What may further distinguish each of us is the degree of honesty and courage we are able to show in looking at our own nature. I believe that the degree to which we are able to see ourselves in the mirror of faith, warts and all, is the degree to which we can appreciate the forgiveness of God through and in Jesus – whose type is Esther – whom we find reflected back to us in that same mirror (Jas. 1:23–25). That you and I are sinners and that we are delivered from the guilt, shame and consequences of that sin by a single representative is the main theme of these comments.

Let us return to Mordecai with these presumptions in mind. I think that there is another purpose in the writer's portrayal of Mordecai, one which allows for a more sympathetic understanding of his role in the story. I believe it is significant that Mordecai's normal station is the king's gate. The frequency of the references to this (2:19–21; 3:2–3; 4:2–6; 5:9–13; 6:10–12) suggest there is more than a historical point or spatial comment being expressed here. It seems to be yet another mechanism that the writer makes use of to underline the theme of access to the king.

Queen Vashti will not go in to the king (1:12) and is, as punishment, denied access thereafter (1:19) on the advice of those described as having special access to the king (1:14). The girl Esther, taken to the king's palace (2:8), moves progressively closer to him before finally making her way to his bed (2:16). Esther is then elevated as queen, the replacement for Vashti, yet still only enjoys access to his presence at his request (4:11). Esther knows that if she is bold enough to approach the king in his inner court unsummoned, she does so at the risk of her life (4:11). Yet it will turn out that it is her access to the king that will be the means of deliverance for her people from potential disaster. This situation was, ironically, brought about by Mordecai's refusal to bow at the gate to Haman, who had been elevated to Prime Minister in his stead and had therefore gained special access to the king (3:1).

The gate is the symbol of access to King Xerxes and is at the heart of the writer's portrayal of events. These are heaped up, one upon another in quick succession, moving seemingly remorselessly to a logical and awful conclusion. Will Esther, on the basis of her relationship with King Xerxes, lord of all the earth, dare to approach him at great personal risk (4:11) on behalf of her people? Will she gain access and favour and deliverance for the people whom she represents, who are under the royal decree of death (3:12–13)? Here is a remarkable pre-fashioning of the story of the mediation of Jesus. Will Esther reverse the consequences of Mordecai's actions, cancel his guilt and deliver her people? Of course, we know the answer – but let us not hurry on too quickly and in doing that not enjoy the telling of the story or the writer's skill in telling it. Indeed the writer will not permit us to do so. Despite the increasing pace of the story, we must feel the tension, the dilemma, the danger and the unlikeliness – indeed the impossibility – of reversing the royal decree if we are truly to celebrate the depth and fullness of that final deliverance.

Will Mordecai, through, with and in Esther, who is uniquely qualified, gain the necessary access to the king who alone can reverse the Jewish fortunes? Will Mordecai obtain the honour and access he might have expected as a result of his actions (2:19–23) in discovering the plot against the king's life? Will his fate under the king's decree be confirmed as a result of his provocation of Haman at the gate? Will he gain access to the throne or will it be denied? For now he remains at the gate and awaits developments. If Mordecai's actions had affected only himself, we might simply be able to dismiss him in his folly and pride and leave him to his fate. But they don't; they drag his entire race down along with him. Furthermore, this is not only a story of one man affecting the destiny of his race. It is also a story, typologically interpreted, of one man affecting the destiny of all humanity. The typology places us with Mordecai at the king's gate. We too await developments – will our provocation, pride, vanity and hypocrisy reap the rewards they deserve or not? Will we find that our expected fate is reversed through our representative? Will we too gain access to the throne? We will have cause at the end of the story to look more closely at this sense of collective identity. It is certainly one of the main points to be drawn from this story.

All Jews are under threat. All Jews celebrate the deliverance accomplished by their representative, Esther. In a similar way, I understand, we, humanity, in some fundamental sense all participate in each other. We all affect one another: our thoughts, words and actions do not merely touch us, or even those in our proximity. The ripples have an impact outward and onward. We are indeed in some deep real way one family, one body. When one suffers we all do, when one is demeaned so are we all, and when one is exalted so are we all. We shall see that as the typology is extended, and as the access gained and favour granted to Queen Esther results in the elevation of Mordecai and the Jews, so the access and favour and its fruits gained by Jesus are extended not simply to all Jews, but to all people.

To return to the story, we have been introduced in 3:1 to Haman, who has been elevated to the closest proximity to the king in Mordecai's place. He is a man very concerned with his own honour, as will be made clear again and again as the story unfolds (3:5; 5:9; 6:6). Because of his desperate insecurity he needs more and more public approval. Yet, despite gaining high honour from the king, he can only see the one person who will not kneel and honour him; he can only hear the one person who will not applaud. We encounter a man who – on the principle that the means used to get to the top will be the means employed to stay at the top – must have been malicious, vain and full of naked ambition in order to reach this position of great political influence and status. We find him totally obsessed with his position and with himself. He has no thought for those whom, we might have thought, he was in that position to serve. Indeed his attitude, and the king's, towards an entire social group (3:15) is very indicative of the heart of the man. We are introduced here to a man who does not hesitate to use the power his position affords to manipulate the weakness and vanity of the king to obtain his own ends, on the pretence that it is to the king's benefit (3:8). His rage (3:5) at a personal affront manifests itself against an entire people, whom the absolute ruler Xerxes puts at his disposal (3:11). This is an ambitious, power-crazed, deceitful, manipulative, lying, hateful, murderous man in a position of power that enables him to do all that the evil of his heart would desire. I want to say three things about this man.

- First, it appears from the story that Esther (4:11) and Haman (6:4) have equivalent access in the inner court of the king. Haman is a depiction for us of the evil one, Satan, who in the next book in the Bible, Job, presents himself in the high court of heaven with a similar evil intent.
- Second, Haman is an incarnation of that evil. We do not have to look too far either in the pages of history or in our own age and century for similar incarnations of evil. With particular reference to the Jews, anyone who has watched the film *Schindler's List* cannot fail to empathize with those who are on the receiving end of the hatred and malice of such a man.
- Third, however, I also want to say that while the foregoing may be true, I believe it is also the case that Haman is far closer to home and to us than we might like to feel, imagine or allow. Wherever there is harm, hurt, injury or abuse – in other words, a victim – there is a perpetrator. Wherever there is a breakdown in a relationship there is responsibility, fault and blame. Who can exclude themselves from the universal participation in this? 'There is no-one righteous, not even one' (Rom. 3:10). 'But anyone who says, "You fool!" will be in danger of the fire of hell' (Mt. 5:22). 'Anyone who looks at a woman lustfully has already committed adultery with her in his heart' (Mt. 5:28). Haman is all of us, but most of us lack the opportunity, power and circumstance that would enable us to act out all the evil that is in our hearts. Before we condemn him too quickly, let us acknowledge our participation in him and he in all of us.

Now, as I have suggested, Mordecai represents every person and our fate hanging in the balance. So, too, are Haman and Esther representatively every person. Whether historical or not, our writer has chosen to 'reveal' the heart of their tale of reversal and deliverance through the rivalry for access to the inner court of the king between the evil man, Haman, and the dependent, weak, submissive, unlikely woman, Esther. Who will triumph? Who will ultimately receive the grace and favour of the king for and on behalf of others? Who will be the servant of all? The female Esther, in seeking access to the king, will be prepared to hazard even her own life for the sake of others (4:11). The male Haman, however, will demonstrate that a leopard cannot change his spots, seeking access to the king not for the sake of others but in order to obtain the death penalty (6:4) for the man whom, ironically, the king seeks to honour (6:10). Does this have something to say about the 'female' side of our humanity, and indeed the 'male' side? Certainly, considering those attributes traditionally associated with the genders, it would appear so. Indeed, does this have something to say about the female side of our deliverer?

Furthermore, as Haman represents humankind intent upon self-glorification, so Esther represents humankind intent upon the service of others. As Haman shows us the nature that will see another hanged, murdered for the sake of wounded pride and vanity, so Esther reveals to us the perfect nature that will risk its own life (4:11) for the sake of others. Our author has chosen to picture for us, in the person of Haman, the first Adam in all his fallenness, so that we may see too in the person of Esther, a woman, the second Adam. We shall see that through the agency of this first Adam the king's decree is against the Jews and is for death. We shall also see that through the agency of the second Adam the equal and opposite decree is for the Jews and is for life (3:12–14; 8:11–13). Our writer, I believe, is pointing us inexorably towards the fullness of the revelation of the mystery made known in Jesus that 'as in Adam all die, so in Christ all will be made alive' (1 Cor. 15:22).

I think I need to take some time out and explain briefly my understanding of the Bible as the means of God's self-revelation. I believe it works in a number of ways which include the following at least.

- First, the Old Testament types – prophet, word, priest, sacrifice, king, servant, judge, and others – are all signs or symbols, icons or windows through which we may look to the fullness made visible (as recorded for us in the gospels) in Jesus.

- Second, each and every type is fulfilled in Jesus, completed in his incarnation, death and resurrection. It is in this way that we may 'see Jesus' (Jn. 12:21) in the whole Bible.

- Third, the nature of this revelation is that it is cumulative. As it unfolds we are able to build up the complete picture made known to us in all its fullness in Jesus (Heb. 1).

- Fourth, as this revelation accumulates and develops I believe that we begin to see a movement away from a more interventionist miracle-working God to a God who accomplishes his purpose by refusing to intervene, by deliberately refusing to perform a miracle and come down from the Cross. Again we see this mirrored in the person, mind and work of Jesus who, it seems to me, gradually moves further and further away from a proclamation of his kingship based on works of power and signs (Jn. 6) to one which is revealed in the breaking of bread and the sharing of a cup of wine. Here I wish to acknowledge Robert Farrar Capon, who has opened this process up for me in his trilogy on the parables of Jesus, comprising: *The Parables of the Kingdom* (1985), *The Parables of Grace* (1988) and *The Parables of Judgment* (1989) (Grand Rapids, MI: William B. Eerdmans).

- Fifth, this revelation is deliberately recorded for us in the form of story. It is not recorded in doctrine, systematic theology or philosophical thoughts, but in relational and personal terms so that even the simplest may receive and encounter. This is again mirrored in the storytelling of Jesus and indeed in his becoming part of the story.

- Sixth, I feel the need to say that this revelation is not capable of being understood: it is a mystery received by faith. I say this deliberately in a western, rationalistic context.

- Seventh, this revelation of the truth of God in his world is paradoxically not received chronologically. By this I mean that I take seriously Jesus' words, 'before Abraham was born, I am'

(Jn. 8:58). The fullness of the revelation made visible in Jesus – and before him in his type, Esther – has always been, is and always will be present (albeit this presence is experienced through absence, is active through God's apparent inactivity and is life bringing and life giving in and through the experience of the valley of the shadow and indeed of death itself). All humankind have always been, will always be and are always in the presence of both Haman and Esther, our representatives in the high court of heaven, and now on earth, in the likeness of whoever we are. Both death (Haman) and life (Esther) and their at-one-ment held out as the promise of deliverance are now, will always be and have always been – often despite appearances – present in this world and to us in one form or another. We shall continue to experience this reality and tension and its reconciliation within ourselves and in our world until that last great day when what has always been true and present will finally be manifest in all eternity. On that day the irreversible law of death will have been reversed through the one full and sufficient sacrifice and oblation for the sins of all, against all and through all time.

While on this tack and before looking at verse 7 in full, let us consider for a moment that once the 'lot' has fallen there is a delay of eleven months before its fulfilment. This does not merely add dramatic tension to this story but also to the story of all history and all our lives. Will we be ready for that fateful day? Even in this respect this small story mirrors all of history and is taken up on the lips of Jesus. The day will come like the visit of a thief in the night (Mt. 24:43), or the arrival of a bridegroom deliberately trying to surprise the waiting bridesmaids (Mt. 25:1–13). How many of us will sit up all night in case a thief should come? How many of us would not want to take part in the bridegroom's game? I believe it is the case that all will be caught out by the thief and not be ready – and yet, in that very unreadiness, that ridiculous virginal precaution of excess oil, all will be made ready in and by him. It is none the less clearly also the case that there will be those who will insist on buying oil rather than taking their chances with such a playful bridegroom. This bridegroom, who knows all along that we would never have enough oil had he not already provided it for us, will be broken-hearted as well as angry at those who will stand self-condemned and exclude themselves from the everlasting banquet. The banquet is the direct result of the deliverance made possible by the second decree. Life is even now present to us, for us and in us if we will only believe, even as we continue to live in a world still obviously under the banner of the first decree, death. God's ultimate verdict in Jesus has, will be and is life, so let us celebrate with this bread and this cup the eternal party of the Lamb.

Having run ahead of ourselves somewhat, let us return to verse 7 and the casting and falling of the 'lot', the *pur* from which the two-day banquet or feast of Purim (9:17–18) got its name. Will it be through luck, coincidence, fate, chance and the misuse of the free will of human beings that God will accomplish his purpose, or will it be through miraculous intervention? Our writer is very definitely of the former viewpoint, which is probably why I warm to their story so much.

It may be merely temperament and personal preference, or it may have some more solid theological footing (which immediately begs the question of why a theological view of truth would be more solid than a personal one – be that as it may), but I have more problems with God's miraculous intervention than with the lack of it. I cannot but pose one question. Why would God apparently intervene in your life and for your benefit and not mine (especially when the crumb of comfort so often volunteered is 'Oh, if you were to have more faith …')? Surely God sends his miracles and blessings on the righteous and unrighteous alike (Mt. 5:45), irrespective of worth, merit or even faith?

My theology of the miraculous is that works of power are signs of a kingdom that works in and through the laying down of power and through the powerless. It is in weakness that we are strong (2 Cor. 12:10) and made perfect (Mt. 5:48). It is on the Cross, life laid down in death, that the power of the gospel and resurrection is to be found. To be taken up with the signs, therefore, is to miss the destination entirely. The reality of the kingdom is a paradox. To seek the sign is to miss that reality. To seek the miraculous, while entirely understandable, is to move away from faith in Jesus, who himself said as much (Mt. 16:4).

But we shall now return to God's non-intervention. Within the ordinary, everyday structure of creation God gives men and women complete freedom to order their own lives. We do so under whatever star sign, fate, religion or rule we choose. Such a god, who will leave us all as free agents, I personally find much easier to cope with than one who will interfere either on behalf of a select few or on a whim or, worse, when certain conditions are fulfilled. Of course, I appreciate that this leaves me with the problem of the unfairness of suffering in the world. This suffering is mitigated to a great extent, in my opinion, by the realization that a very significant proportion of it is not the responsibility of a god who lacks compassion but the responsibility of humankind, who will not steward the more than adequate resources available in an equitable manner.

All of this is not to say that there is no order in creation. There is. It is not to say that our world is only characterized by chaos, luck, chance or accident or that there is no such thing as cause and effect. Of course there is. There are norms, rules with which we can choose to co-operate or not. Just as gravity holds everything to the planet, so relationships break in the face of a lack of truth, trust, faithfulness and kindness. There is also a further paradoxical order in our world that is illustrated in the story of Esther. Our expectations are, more often than not, surprisingly reversed with the last coming first and vice versa. This is both wonderful and disconcerting, depending of course on whether one is first or last.

All of this is to say that the means by which God – in the sovereign laying down of his power – accomplishes his equally sovereign determination to deliver all humankind is both through a remarkable reversal and through the very luck and chance that is delightfully and irritatingly characteristic of this created order. I must also say that the freedom God gives us to choose how we will respond to him, to this created order and the luck of how our particular cookie crumbles generally leads us, individually and

collectively, to the drainpipe of history. In our freedom, we all
seem determined to pour ourselves down this drainpipe. We
know that very often buttered toast covered with jam will, when
dropped, fall face down on the carpet. Is it not also the case that
it sometimes lands jam-side-up? There is both a goodness to creation and a twistedness, not to mention that element of luck.
God has not only ordered this creation, but more remarkably he
still submits himself to accomplishing his purpose by working
within it. Is it not the case that we could all say 'Amen' ('I agree';
'Yes, that is true') to the words 'well, fancy that!'? We never
really know what's round the corner. Things go on turning up for
good and ill, unexpectedly calling forth and demanding that we
respond. Despite Haman's (and our) endeavours, following the
casting of the lot, to harness and control by law the fall of the die
on a certain day, it is by its very nature uncontrollable.

At the feast of Purim Judaism celebrates the chance, fate and
luck of the drawing of the lot and the casting of the die ultimately
in their favour, despite the intention of Haman, the rule of law,
the structure of society and the apparent hopelessness of their
circumstance. They celebrate the reality that God chooses these
very means in order to accomplish their deliverance. All for what
purpose? That we, who in the exercise of our freedom have pro-
voked our need of deliverance, may still be free on the day that
deliverance is manifest to respond to the one who has delivered
us. He has delivered us without our assistance and indeed often
in the face of our resistance. He is the one who has not only been
our mediator but the very means of that mediation; the one who
did not merely risk his life, but laid it down that we all might live.
To this response we shall turn in the next chapter.

4

Mordecai Approaches Esther

I trust you will not only know but also appreciate the form by now and will already have read chapter 4. The wider historical and cultural context has been set in chapter 1. The more narrowly defined and particular context of the king's palace and Esther's place in it were established in chapter 2. In chapter 3 the plot emerged, in the antagonism between Mordecai the Jew and Haman the descendant of Agag, and the decree of King Xerxes that on the fateful day indicated by the casting of the lot all Jews in the known world would be doomed. From chapter 4 through to chapter 8 the tension grows, the pace quickens and the action in the palace intensifies. The key player is Esther, who will continue throughout to develop and mature as a woman, a queen and a deliverer.

Mordecai, in occupying his place at the king's gate (4:2,6), no longer deliberately provokes Haman (3:2,5), the Prime Minister with direct access to the king, but tries to attract the attention of another with similar access, Queen Esther (4:4). He has now realized that his provocation of Haman has not only brought him but his entire race into great danger (3:13). The weakness of the absolute ruler, King Xerxes, combined with the malice and vanity in Haman, seem to have brought Mordecai to his senses. Michael V. Fox comments, 'genuine grief and agitation are natural reactions in a man whose people has been threatened with annihilation' (p. 57). I would add that Mordecai's identification with his people in his reaction (4:1,3) might be motivated by fear of their reaction to him and certainly, as I have discussed, lays him open to the charge of hypocrisy.

His actions, clothing and attitude at the king's gate may be merely those of a genuine penitent without premeditation, but I do not think so. Mordecai seems to have a deliberate plan in mind in seeking to attract Esther's attention (4:6–8). Esther is very clear that this further public demonstration by Mordecai is dangerous. She sends him clothes (4:4) in an attempt to limit the damage and to find out (4:5) the cause of his distress. J.D. Levenson (p. 79) makes the point that the gulf 'between Mordecai the Jew and Esther the Persian' is firmly established. I agree, but it seems to me that our writer, in not criticizing Esther's adaptation to the court, is continuing to establish the purpose, method and benefit of such adaptation as an acceptable way for non-returning Jewish exiles to live. The writer is fully conscious of the contrast of Esther's situation with the Jewish separatism of Mordecai, which not only fails to serve the purpose of deliverance but has actually predicated and precipitated the destruction of the Jews. What this has to say about our writer's view of the more general separatist attitude of not only Jewish but also Christian history I trust I do not have to spell out any further.

M.V. Fox comments (pp. 58–9), 'While Mordecai is displaying his grief in one of the most visible spots in the kingdom, and Jews throughout the kingdom are fasting and lamenting, Esther, cloistered in luxury, remains oblivious to the uproar … the meaning and cause of Mordecai's behaviour does not seem to have mattered to her.' I would not agree with this view. Not only has Mordecai precipitated the very cause of his (now penitent) behaviour, but Esther, we are told explicitly, does not know about the decree against the Jews (4:5), presumably as a result of her being cut off from society at large inside the king's harem. She seeks to find out the reason for Mordecai's grief (4:5), takes responsibility (4:16) and – despite the danger – immediately decides on her course of action. Mordecai's plan for her to break the law (4:11) in approaching the king directly is precisely the kind of legal disobedience that brought this danger upon them in the first place. In addition, Mordecai's public display of grief is neither the action of a Jewish separatist hero like Daniel, who retreated to his private room (Dan. 6:10), nor that of the Jewish deliverer to come who encourages us not to make a display but likewise to go to our room and pray, 'for your Father knows what you need before you ask him' (Mt. 6:5–8).

In my view it is Esther, not Mordecai, whom our writer is seeking to put forward as a pattern for our behaviour and as an example of faith. Her wisdom is sensible and pragmatic and I believe it is the very wisdom of God that is made known to us in her, as she is a type of Jesus. The fasting (4:3,16) can be viewed, I believe, instructively, from the point of view of Jesus' words in Matthew 6:16–18.

Private wisdom and faith (4:16) are contrasted with public display (4:1–2) and self-seeking (4:13). Sackcloth and ashes (4:1) are exchanged for robes of royalty (6:9) and the movement between honour and dishonour and vice versa is evident in both Haman and Mordecai (3:1–2; 7:9; 9:13; 9:25). Mordecai is not initially honoured for his actions (2:19–23) but is honoured belatedly (6:11). He is not only delivered from the public death planned for him by his enemy Haman (5:14; 6:10) but also replaces him in the most elevated public office of all – that of Prime Minister (8:2). This without doubt forms the core of our writer's understanding of the nature of deliverance: the reversal of circumstances. Private fear, secrecy, danger, fasting and the threat of death are replaced by public recognition, openness, security, joy and life.

This deliverance – a change in fortune and consequent freedom – and the subsequent public uninhibited celebration are themselves the direct result of the most intimate and private access gained by Esther to the inner court of absolute ruler King Xerxes, in the face of the law of unapproachability (4:11). As the representative of her people, Esther gains access to the throne, defeats Haman and reverses his evil plan. The typology seems so obvious and so clear to me that it is surely the wisdom of God made known to us – albeit in very irreligious clothes.

We shall now turn to a brief consideration of the use our writer makes of clothing as a symbol of attitude and status. King Xerxes (1:4) publicly displays 'the vast splendour and glory of his majesty'. Queen Vashti is ordered to dress (1:11) so as to 'display her beauty to the people and nobles'. A royal crown is given to Esther to wear (2:17). Mordecai and the Jews (4:1,3) wear sackcloth and Esther sends Mordecai clothes (4:4) to cover himself. It is when she is dressed in her royal robes that Queen Esther dares to approach Xerxes (5:1). Mordecai's honour (6:11) is displayed with royal robes (6:8,9; 8:15). The tradition of dressing up for the retelling of the story of Esther at their annual feast of Purim is maintained by Jews to this day.

Our clothes do not simply indicate our station or reflect our mood, or even symbolize a change in status or attitude, though both of these are clearly part of the way our writer uses clothes to tell their story. Our clothes are a shop window to our hearts; they are an important reflection of our image and who we are. This is not merely a 'rags to riches' story with its inverse reflection thrown in for good measure. There is a further dimension, which I would term sacramental. It is not just that in approaching the king (5:1) or in being honoured by the king (6:7–9) we wear special clothes, but that in so doing and by such honour we are identified with the one whose clothes we wear. Once again the typology seems clear. Those who have been delivered are clothed with their deliverer – the Lord Jesus Christ (Rom. 13:14; Col. 3:9–10). They are in him (Gal. 3:27), and participate in his honour, splendour and majesty (1:4).

I am aware that this argument may reach too far for some, but it will not be in our own dirty clothes (sinfulness) and certainly not in our best clothes (self-righteousness [Zech. 3:4]) that we shall approach the eternal throne. We shall be in the clothes supplied by the king (Mt. 22:11–12), the very righteousness of Christ (Rom. 3:21–24), available to all by faith, the mere touch of which brings salvation and deliverance (Mk. 5:28). The symbolism of clothing reflects nothing less than the change in status or fortune from mortality to eternal life (1 Cor. 15:54; 2 Cor. 5:2) for all those who are in Christ Jesus, the king's son – both the good and the bad (Mt. 22:10).

We have now looked in some detail at the window of clothing, which is yet another way in which our writer seeks to symbolize the meaning and manifestation of their theme – deliverance, a

change in fortune from dishonour to honour and elevation from
the secret and private realm to public display. This deliverance is
accomplished and displayed in the royal personage of Esther. I
believe our author deliberately casts Esther, a woman, as heroine
over and against Mordecai, the more expected and likely male
candidate for the role. It seems to me that this must say something very important to us about our understanding of Esther, a
female type of the man, the deliverer, Jesus Christ.

We must now return to Mordecai to examine his motivation
in making an appeal to his ward, the queen. I am sure his heart
and motivation are mixed, as indeed are ours all too often.
Perhaps I am overreacting to the merits attributed to him by most
commentators, but I am convinced that our author is underlining
the point that it is not through his merits, his clothes and his righteousness that deliverance can be accomplished, let alone risked.
Deliverance is always a perilous business and in the Bible neither
Israel in the shape of her representative, Mordecai, nor humanity
in the shape of theirs, Adam (both men) is allowed to feel any
self-confidence in approaching the absolute ruler of heaven and
earth. Not only are we not righteous, we are in our pride and
vanity deliberately and provocatively unrighteous. If there is to
be deliverance for Mordecai and those identified with him, the
Jews (and indeed for Adam and those identified with him, all
humankind), then it must be granted by another and must be the
result of the righteous actions of someone else. We always have
and always will need someone else to mediate our deliverance to
and for us.

Mordecai, it seems to me, tries a number of tactics in order to
persuade Esther (4:8) to act on her people's behalf. I am not sure
that she needed such persuasion. We shall examine her motivation and possible alternative responses to Mordecai, and her circumstances, later. Mordecai seems to me not dissimilar to the
prodigal son, who in rehearsing his speech as he journeys home
(Lk. 15:18–19) finds himself cut off in mid-sentence by his
advancing father (Lk. 15:21–24). His father is not to be bar-
gained with or bought, and thereby misunderstood, but will be
seen to be moved purely out of love and compassion for this son

who was lost but is now found, who was dead but is now alive again (Lk. 15:32).

Let us list the means this man Mordecai uses to try to twist the arm of the deliverer, Esther (4:13–14).

- First, he appeals to Esther on the basis of his authority as her legal guardian (2:7), a tactic that had ensured her obedience previously (2:10). Presumably he understands her being 'in the king's house' (4:13) as a great benefit and a direct result of his wisdom, counsel and direction.
- Second, he reminds her of the name of her 'father's family' (4:14) and the duty owed to their memory.
- Third, he appeals to her basic instinct for self-preservation or, to put this perhaps more callously, the same selfishness that characterizes him (4:13).
- Fourth, he amplifies this instinct, perhaps by projecting his own character and motivation on to Esther, trying to induce fear: 'Do not think ... you alone of all the Jews will escape [death under the decree]' (4:13).
- Fifth, he tries to shame Esther: 'if you remain silent at this time, relief and deliverance for the Jews will arise from another place' (4:14).
- Sixth, he attempts to induce guilt in Esther by suggesting that she may be responsible for the death of all the Jews if she does not take up the opportunity of having 'come to royal position for such a time as this' (4:14).
- Last, and here he seems to want to have his cake and eat it, he tries flattery. He approaches her not as his ward but as queen. He wants to take advantage of her 'royal position' in the 'king's house' (4:13–14).

Now, I appreciate that these motives may be interpreted more positively. Mordecai's first and second appeals to duty, based upon his authority, could truly be the fruits of his family love for her and for their family ties. His third and fourth attempts appeal to an inherent selfishness and fear, and could be fatherly advice to a daughter not fully aware of the peril of her own situation.

His fifth attempt, to shame Esther, could in fact be a statement of his great faith in God the deliverer, who will act with or without the co-operation of Esther. His sixth attempt, to induce guilt, could be nothing more than practical wisdom, and his seventh approach, that of flattery, may actually be him appropriately and humbly honouring her royal position as queen.

I have given my reasons for believing that our writer directs us to the less creditable list of motives, but it is also the case that one's motivation is rarely simply of one kind. Without giving Mordecai too much credit, therefore, we can attribute a variety to him. Certainly, with his mission accomplished, Mordecai rather ironically 'went away and carried out all of Esther's instructions' (4:17). The boot is very firmly on the other foot now; the roles are reversed and perhaps Mordecai has come to his senses and seen that his way (4:8) was not the wisest. Esther's plan (to be unfolded in chapters 5 – 8), which will rely on patient, sensitive submission and on choosing the 'right' moment and the 'right' manner of approach to the king, is extremely courageous and couldn't, as we shall see, be more successful.

We must now look at Esther's responses to Mordecai's plea (4:8). J.D. Levenson (p. 79) sees, I believe correctly, a number of analogies between the respective roles of Esther and Mordecai in our story and those of Moses and Aaron. As Esther is to Xerxes, so Moses is to Pharaoh, but whereas Moses fails to persuade Pharaoh and God's intervention is crucial, Esther succeeds. Like Moses, Esther must decide whether or not to be identified with God's people. Like Moses, Esther has a number of possible courses of action open to her. She might do any of the following:

1 Seek to maintain the secrecy of her identity and in this way avoid the ethnic cleansing – is she her 'brother's keeper?' (Gen. 4:9).
2 Seek to excuse herself either on the basis of gender, or on the basis that her royal position could not be abused (as opposed to an inability to speak in public – an excuse used by Moses in Exodus 4:10).

3 Seek to avoid the responsibility of her position by pleading either that the mission is truly impossible since the law is irreversible or, alternatively, since she has not been called to the king's bedchamber for thirty days (4:11), that her access to the king is too dangerous and therefore the chance of success is severely limited.

4 Obey Mordecai, as before, and go to the king as instructed (4:8).

5 Fast and pray, and seek the wisdom of others. The only likely source of such wisdom, apart from Mordecai, would be the king's eunuchs in the harem (2:8–9), though they might not be considered a particularly reliable source of wisdom, as the king himself is known to seek and take their counsel (7:9).

6 Trust that deliverance would indeed be forthcoming from another place (4:14).

7 Approach the king, not in obedience to Mordecai, but in an attitude of faith: 'if I perish, I perish' (4:16).

As it is with Mordecai, so it is with Esther. It is likely that she experienced a mixture of motives. It would be very natural for her to experience both positive and negative motives: reluctance, duty, fear and courage. The film *Schindler's List* provides a helpful and instructive insight into how a modern-day counterpart to Moredcai and Esther, Oskar Schindler, responded in a similar context. I would not wish to be quick to condemn anyone, perhaps excepting the self-congratulatory and self-righteous. There will always be those who are overwhelmed by fear and paralysed into inaction, or who are motivated only by self-preservation in the face of violence, hatred, malice and evil.

From a typological perspective, however, I believe that we must contrast the purity of Esther's 'motivation' – the selflessness of her action, the nature of her status and the uniqueness of her access to the inner court of the king – with the person, motivation, attitude and action of Mordecai. In my mind, the writer portrays only one agent of deliverance, only one mediator, and only one suitably qualified royal personage who can and who will voluntarily put themselves under the threat of death for the sake of others.

Esther does not excuse herself. In taking seriously her relationship with and access to the king, as well as her representative role to her people, she acts decisively. In this response we can see development in the person and character of Esther. She is no longer the obedient girl; she has indeed 'won his favour and approval' (2:17). She is thinking, and, as we shall see, planning and acting independently of Mordecai on behalf of her people. She has become a woman, a queen and a deliverer. She very quickly (4:15) decides how she will act and exhibits great courage and faith in the face of adversity and, let it be underlined, of loneliness. She alone must approach the king.

It is usual to understand the three-day fast (4:16) as a religious rite, whereby implicitly Esther and her people will put their trust in Yahweh, their God, presumably not to harden Xerxes' heart as he had hardened Pharaoh's heart (Ex. 7:3). While I believe that such faith and trust is implicit in our text, I none the less maintain that, rather than this fast being a specifically religious rite, it is a demonstration of earnestness and commitment proportionate to, and in preparation for, the seriousness of the undertaking before her. It gives Esther the necessary time to focus on her objective, those for whom she will act and the God in whom she will trust, as well as to give consideration to the request she must make, not to mention the danger. I do not think this fast is intended by our writer to be understood in narrowly religious terms. I am sure that if that were their intention, they would have told us that the request included prayer. The narrative deliberately and strangely makes no mention of prayer. This obvious secularization of the story of deliverance has offended commentators ever since it was written. They have long noted the avoidance of religious language, observance and rite and even of the name of God.

My contention in this 'commentary' is that in the book of Esther we have reached a decisive point in the progressive and cumulative revelation of God. This book immediately precedes the centuries of silence that are to be followed by the final supreme revelation of God in the person of his son (Heb. 1:2). It is, I believe, therefore making a number of deliberate statements:

1 The new deliverance will not be accomplished by a mighty intervention.
2 It will be accomplished not only through the chance and fate of this life but also at the bottom of the drainpipe of history to which the abuse of our freedom inevitably leads.
3 While this is all true, it remains the case that God is committed to the deliverance of his people.
4 While the means may seem different, the end is a complete fulfilment of the broader biblical revelation of sacred history and its typology.
5 Accommodation in this world, not separation, is the way for the people of God to live.
6 To trust in a visible, ritualistic religion such as that to which Israel in her history has succumbed is condemned.
7 It is by faith that we trust in the invisible hand of an invisible God whose deliverance is mysterious, who reverses all our expectations, and who is hidden from us.

I believe that the book of Esther provides an alternative view of God. Here is a God who, rather than answering the cries of his people by intervening on their behalf, accomplishes his purpose invisibly and answers their prayers for deliverance by entering into their reality himself, by going down into the disaster of their history with them, and then and only then raising them to life with him.

I want now to conclude this chapter firstly by looking at one attempt to find God in this book that does not resort to apocryphal additions, and secondly by saying something about the place, nature, role, purpose and meaning of prayer.

J. Sidlow Baxter in his work *Explore the Book* (Grand Rapids, MI: Zondervan, 1960, p. 261) finds the name of God 'hidden' in acrostic form in the Hebrew text of Esther five times (1:20; 5:4,13; 7:5–7). That God's name, YeHoVaH, is 'hidden' mirrors the point made by the narrative itself. It is in this very hiddenness that 'in all things God works for the good of those who love him' (Rom. 8:28), and despite the intended harm, God intended it for good, to accomplish his purpose, 'the saving of many lives' (Gen. 50:20).

I believe that Sidlow Baxter's theology is correct; that the greatest miracle of deliverance is that of not resorting to a miracle in order to accomplish it. The mightiest miracle is that the invisible hand of God none the less accomplishes his loving purpose of deliverance for his people. In the face of our great determination to thwart that purpose and deny that deliverance, God wills us life and not death. Despite our determination to set our corporate and individual face against him, he accomplishes deliverance and then awaits our response in love. God's is indeed a blessed resistance to us. I reserve judgement about whether the name of God was truly intentionally hidden in this book, either by the writer or by the Holy Spirit, and about whether it is really there or even necessary.

Lastly, let us give some brief consideration to prayer. It will be brief because prayer is to do with a private, subjective relationship of love with almighty God. The apostle Paul prays that the Ephesians may grasp how wide, long, high and deep the love of Christ is, asking that they might 'be filled to the measure of all the fullness of God' (Eph. 3:18–19).

The reason for this brief consideration of prayer is the lack of mention of it in the story of Esther at any point, and most especially at the point of crisis. If my experience is anything to go by, there is nothing like impending trauma to elicit a desperate cry to God for help. The silence of the book of Esther on this matter, as well as Esther's personal avoidance of any religious language and anything cultic, is therefore deafening.

As we have seen, our author is committed to revealing the work of God in delivering his people without resort to miraculous intervention. They are committed to demonstrating God's sovereignty and power in accomplishing his purpose by showing that he not only permits any and all human activity – including malice aforethought – but oversees history so that accident, coincidence, chance, luck and fate all combine to secure that purpose.

I believe that our author wants to show that Esther is an ordinary human being. But they also want to show us that Esther is a unique deliverer, mediator and royal representative of her people, set apart from all others for service.

It is not that our author does not believe that God answers prayer, nor even that they intend to discourage us from praying. Our author, in believing in God as a God of deliverance who reverses fortunes (as evidenced by the second edict celebrated in perpetuity at the feast of Purim), knows that there will always be a need for an Esther. Circumstances will not only be unchanged at the end of the book, but will also persistently demonstrate themselves to be irreversible in the experience of the faithful, whether they pray or not. This may seem depressing, despairing and hopeless. It isn't, so please read on.

- First, though there will be many an occasion when deliverance will not be forthcoming, however desperate the circumstances, however faithful the prayer, our author believes that there will be an ultimate eschatological deliverance in which we may have complete confidence.
- Second, there will be many an occasion when deliverance is forthcoming in desperate circumstances when there has been no resort to prayer either by those who call themselves believers or those who do not.
- Third, in the light of much hard evidence both in the sacred and secular history of deliverance – both in answer to prayer and as a result of a chain of coincidences, accidents, strokes of luck and 'well fancy thats' – our author encourages us to believe in God whether or not we perish (4:16). The grand metanarrative of every individual and of all history is that God is determined to change our fortunes and bring about our deliverance.
- Fourth, prayer is ultimately only 'true' prayer if it is in accordance with God's will and not ours (Mt. 26:39). It is in Gethsemane that we finally and most fully see Jesus' answer to the disciples' request that he should teach them how to pray (Lk. 11:1). Whatever we may think is best, whatever we may want,

in the end prayer is a conformity of our will to his. Whatever we may wish, whatever we might prefer, that will is not deliverance from the Cross but on it. While there may be many blessings and even answers along the way, ultimately what will be will be, and what will be is the assurance of God's presence, love and deliverance – though, as we see supremely in the person of Jesus on the Cross, it certainly won't always feel like it: 'My God, my God, why have you forsaken me?' (Mk.15:34).

- So, fifth, and perhaps most wonderfully of all, our author leads us in a particular direction. It is in the cast of the lot, in the face of fate and of the evil that would apply and misuse it and the power that would give it the irreversible force of law; it is in the consequence of accident, coincidence, luck, law, abuse of power and evil – namely death – that God chooses to meet us and to raise us up with him to life everlasting.

- Sixth, there is the goal and answer to prayer: the unity of our will with his. Typologically, intimacy with Yahweh ('I am' with you and for you always) has already been given to us in and through Queen Esther. In the exemplar Esther, who gained access and broke down the wall of hostility between those she represented and King Xerxes, we already have access to God and his peace with our neighbour and ourselves (Eph. 2:14). It is not that we go on needing to pray and seeking his presence: he has found us and will never let us go.

- So, seventh and lastly, prayer is the desire that we might know his will and be found by him, be identified with Esther in his presence, and experience deliverance through death. The prayer that will most assuredly be permanently answered, always and everywhere, is that we may *now* taste death, we may *now* walk in the way of the Cross, we may *now* be last, least and humbled and, in so losing our life, may *now* taste life, resurrection, elevation and exaltation. As we go on celebrating with the bread and the cup we may indeed be the broken, the poured out, yet at the same time the blessed and distributed body of Christ. Paradoxically then, our author could not offer us a stronger encouragement to pray than if Esther herself had prayed. But notice that in seeking and gaining access to King Xerxes, in conforming her will to his for and on behalf of her people at the risk of her own life, and in accomplishing the means of their deliverance, not only did Esther pray, she was prayer. Jesus likewise was prayer, and so in him may we be.

5

Esther Approaches the King

I think that you may be feeling the need for some theological explanation. When the sermon series I offered on this subject reached this point, some anxiety was being voiced. It was along the following lines. If God allows us complete freedom and does not ordinarily intervene miraculously, then:

1 How can we maintain that he is a loving heavenly father who cares for his children?
2 What do signs and wonders mean?
3 Why should we bother praying?
4 What is the point in being a Christian believer?

I know it sounds as though I have defined deliverance as precisely its opposite – namely, a lack of deliverance. Moreover I have come to this conclusion from a story which explicitly, if non-miraculously, proclaims a very definite deliverance from the direst of circumstances. I would truly like things to be simpler, but I am afraid they are not. The gospel is a paradox and a mystery. If we are to enter the kingdom of heaven we must be 'like a little child' (Mk. 10:15). Jesus himself, on another occasion, gave thanks that this mystery had been hidden 'from the wise and learned, and revealed ... to little children' (Mt. 11:25). We must take Jesus' words seriously. We cannot understand the mystery of the gospel, but we can struggle to be held by God's self-revelation. This book is an attempt to read the story of Esther through the fullness of its revelation – Jesus Christ. At one level the story can be understood very simply. God – though not sought, let alone mentioned – delivers his people, even though they are disobedient and have remained in exile, from their enemies and oppressors. Without resorting to extraordinary intervention and using only the ordinary exigencies of life to accomplish his sovereign purpose (Rom. 8:28), God providentially delivers his people.

However, not only from the perspective of the New Testament, but also from that of the rest of the Old Testament covenant history, this story is only superficially simple. How is it that Israel, who were ultimately punished and exiled for disobedience and unfaithfulness, could experience God's blessing, let alone his deliverance? Stranger still, how could this also be true for those Jews not returning from exile? Why would God bless them in this way, particularly when he wasn't even asked to do so? Was Cyrus the Persian really the Messiah of God (Is. 45:1)? Are Persians outside the covenant? Doesn't God normally demonstrate his side of the covenant by leaving his people in no doubt that it is his mighty arm alone that accomplishes deliverance, without any possibility of co-operative effort? Is God's sovereign covenant purpose the deliverance of Israel alone, or does he want a relationship with all humankind (Gen. 1:27; 9:16; 12:3)? This is certainly not a simple story.

Whatever our theology, we have questions that we do not have an answer for. The four questions outlined at the beginning of the chapter are the major ones that occurred to the congregation at St Paul's in Cambridge as we struggled with my Christological understanding of the story, Sunday by Sunday. It was this questioning approach to the story, together with a total conviction of the unity in diversity and the authority of all Scripture, that led me to my conclusions.

If Esther is a type for Jesus, as I believe, what does this tell us about him and the gospel of deliverance? If God did not intervene miraculously for the deliverance of his people, yet still accomplished that very thing, what does this tell us about Jesus, the gospel of deliverance, and indeed our heavenly father? If the circumstances of God's people are unchanged at the end of the story, in the sense that they have continued to be an oppressed and persecuted minority throughout history, what does this tell us about the meaning and content of the gospel and how God accomplishes his purpose in and through Jesus? If in the Jewish Jesus God's covenant with his people is fulfilled, is it not also true that in Jesus the man God's covenant is fulfilled with all humankind? What does this say about the enemies of God's people in our story?

It is this Christological prior commitment to this short story about Jewish deliverance, and the subsequent typological understanding, that have led me to believe that it is precisely in his inactivity that God demonstrates his compassion and love most fully. It is through non-intervention that God accomplishes his covenant purpose, delivers his people, and ultimately their enemies too. He does this in and through Jesus, whose type is Esther.

So we can return to our four questions.

1 How can we maintain that God is a loving heavenly father who cares for his children if he does not intervene?

The deliverance God will accomplish must be fair to all his people, and it must be equally accessible if his covenant stands both with all Israel and with all humankind. Further, if we are determined – as the evidence would indicate – to pour ourselves down the drainpipe of history, then God must, if he wishes a free response in allowing us the freedom to do so, accomplish his purpose at the bottom of that drainpipe. Patching up, band aids, healings along the way are one thing, but ultimately we must be delivered from the 'big one' – death. This is where God must meet us if deliverance is to be real. God will not infringe upon our freedom and out of love will allow us, like adolescents, to know best and to walk away. Out of his desperate love he pleads, weeps and waits for us as we consistently fall into every pot-hole in the way and finally into the grave-hole of death. Along the way he also provides for us innumerable blessings and good things as well as those coincidences, strokes of luck, accidents and good fortune that seem to be part of the way he has constructed his creation, which continues to be very good (Gen. 1:31). These blessings and this provision are not given only to a select few: the sun shines on the righteous and the unrighteous alike. In creation, as well as in deliverance, God loves everyone and everything. He has no favourites, unless that includes all of us.

God by his non-intervention in our lives is fair to all his children. In meeting us all in our most desperate need, Jesus died, and, in Jesus' resurrection he raises us all to the promised deliverance.

2 What do signs and wonders mean if God does not intervene?

Signs and wonders are given to direct our attention to him, the giver, and so that we may wonder at his generosity, compassion and love. They are given that we may know he is God, almighty to deliver. They are focused in deliverance and direct our attention there. They must be understood in the light of his character and purpose and ultimately as the means by which he accomplishes our deliverance – by not delivering Jesus from the Cross.

To anticipate miracles as an everyday occurrence seems to me to deny what they are by definition: out of the ordinary. It also directs our attention away from the much more paradoxical and far less obvious truth that God calls all of us to trust him, particularly in the face of a complete lack of miracle in death. Of course, he will remain faithful to us whether we are faithful or not, and, on the other side of his failure to deliver us miraculously from death, he will raise us up to a new order of reality: life in eternity.

God gives the extraordinary to confirm both his determination and his ability to deliver us, in order that we might trust him in the ordinary when there is no miraculous intervention. The impossibility of the miracles Jesus performed demonstrates this. It is precisely because the blind see, the lame walk, the deaf hear, the prisoners are released and the dead are raised that we may believe that sinners are forgiven, and that in Jesus deliverance is already a reality. I believe that it is not God's intention that we seek miraculous intervention but that we trust him when there is none. My reading of the gospels suggests that initially there was an abundance of miracles, inevitably misunderstood (Jn. 6:14–15). These gradually decreased with the ultimate revelation of the miracle of the deliverance of God – resurrection and eternal life, not 'out of' disaster but 'in it', not 'down from' the Cross but 'on it'. It is my conviction that God no more promises to keep us in the best of times than he promises to rescue us from the worst. He simply promises to be with us always – whether we believe it, feel it, experience it, understand it or not.

3 Why should we bother praying if God will not intervene or answer?

I have tried to outline my understanding of prayer in the previous chapter. Someone recently asked me, 'Why do you pray?' If God is a loving heavenly father, knowing what we need before we ask, if he loves to give, does not need vain repetition and has more than enough power to provide all I need, why should we bother? Alternatively, if God merely lets the world get on with itself (please understand this in the light of his divine oversight, compassion, purpose and structuring of creation for our good and for our deliverance), then it seems that there is no point in praying. Logically, whichever view one takes, the question remains: why pray? If God were to answer, then I might be tempted to focus on the pre-conditions. If God answered someone else and not me, wouldn't that be unfair? If God didn't answer, where would that leave me?

For ten years, throughout the infancy of our four children, I prayed for a night's sleep. On about six occasions, God answered. This experience has given me more than sufficient cause to examine my understanding of God's commitment to answering my prayer. My answer to question three, apart from 'It's a mystery; I don't know' is 'Jesus did'. Now this, it seems to me, holds the key to the mystery of prayer. God's will, not mine, is for my deliverance. While he may or may not send signs and wonders in answer to prayer, his will is to direct me to that will. He wills that I trust him. His will is that my experience and my prayer might gradually conform my will to his. His will is that I believe he has already, in Jesus Christ crucified, accomplished the deliverance of all creation (including me), not by avoiding the downward spiral of history but by going down with it. He will no more take this cup from us than he took it from Jesus (Mt. 26:39). Paradoxically it is in drinking that very cup to the full that we experience fullness of life. Whether God intervenes and answers specific prayers in time and place, over and against all the sociological, psychological, emotional and other variables, I reserve judgement. That he wills for us to participate voluntarily in and to drink the reality of his deliverance to the full, I can only glimpse, wonder, give thanks for and praise.

4 What is the point in being a Christian believer if God does not intervene on a Christian's behalf?

If God loves even his enemies and blesses us whether we seek him or not, won't interfere when we need or want him to but will just allow things to happen, and if our deliverance is already accomplished in Jesus, then what is the point in being a Christian believer?

Now this, it seems to me, is the easiest of the four questions in this theological trawl to deal with. This, to me, has the feel of the parable of the workers in the vineyard (Mt. 20:1–16). Perhaps I am being unfair, but the root, I believe, of this question is this. God is very lucky to have me as a Christian. I expect a reward for all the effort I have put into being a Christian and living 'righteously'. Far more insidiously, there is a feeling that God ought to deal in the other way – by punishment and hell (though I might not articulate this) – for those who are either not Christian or not good.

Let me deal with this positively first. All of us, every human being, has already been rewarded with the grace of eternal life not only in creation but in the deliverance of Christ. Nothing we do – or rather all the good we don't, haven't, can't, won't do – matters a row of beans to God, who has clothed us in Christ with his deliverance and his righteousness. The reason for being a

Christian, for going to church and for being good is not to twist God's arm. It is not one-upmanship, nor is it an insurance policy against disaster (the worst has already happened and miraculously the insurance company have paid out in full, even though we hadn't paid the premiums). It is not to earn a full day's pay. God will pay us our wages if we demand them (Rom. 6:23). If we will only dare to believe that he already paid Jesus then we might begin to dare to believe that the immeasurably better thing, life, a free gift, is already in our possession. The reason for being a Christian is to celebrate all that he has already given and more, and especially to celebrate God the giver, and Jesus Christ, in whom he gives us all things.

Expressing this negatively, the question has to do with this. Why should we have suffered the requirements of the Christian religion if God gives the benefits freely to everyone? The answer is that there is no reason. If this is why you are a Christian, why you are good or come to church – as I say to my congregation often – don't come, don't do it, stop. Please don't think you are doing God any favours by being a miserable, jealous, bitter, sad, religious Christian practitioner. He wills you to celebrate. So do yourself a favour, give up on religion, even on the Christian religion. Your deliverance has nothing to do with your behaviour, works or goodness, let alone your religion. It doesn't even have a great deal to do with your faith, particularly if you have turned that into another work or an intellectual or doctrinal test. It has all to do with God, his grace, and his deliverance of you, which is already accomplished. Once we begin to see this we can stop worrying, begin trusting, and enjoy all God's goodness. We can give thanks and meet freely together to celebrate this life that is ours only and always through Jesus Christ. And why be good? That is simple: goodness is its own reward. God has made all things good. If we live in line with the structure of creation, if we are faithful, kind and true in relationships, who knows but we might enjoy all the abundance God intends for us in this life. When we lie, cheat, steal, manipulate and deceive we know what results, but he has warned us about that. As I have already discussed, this is not foolproof, toast does not always land jam-side-up, accidents do happen, but creation is still good – very good.

Now, having cleared, I hope helpfully, some of the theological ground cover, let us return to the plot and chapter 5 of Esther. Please do read it. As the representative of her people, Esther, having prepared herself by a three-day fast (cf. twelve months' beauty treatment –1:12) and having put on royal vestments, dares to approach the king. Will he extend his sceptre or have her put to death? Will he look upon her and her request with favour or not? She is a type of Christ and typologically the whole destiny of humankind hangs in the balance of this encounter between the lord of all, Xerxes, and Esther, the woman, the would-be deliverer.

We watched *Sleepless in Seattle* as a family recently (can it really rain that much there?). Now, because this was Hollywood, we all anticipated and collectively greeted the tearful end to the film. We, the viewers, felt we needed and deserved such an ending, but is life like that? Will Sam and Annie meet? It seems most unlikely, though as viewers we know they will. They live on opposite sides of the continent. The possibility has only come about because of a ridiculous radio phone-in; the naïvety of Sam's son, Jonah; the practicality of Jonah's friend, Jessica; the coincidence of the letter, sent without permission, being read; the replaying of that ancient tale of love conquering all (with Cary Grant and Deborah Kerr); the symbol of the Empire State Building; the unlikeliness of either party daring to believe in this film/dream/tale; and finally, to cap it all, the fated 'coincidence' of their meeting when all had seemed lost, because Jonah just happened to forget his rucksack. Brilliant!

We, of course, know the end of our story of Esther, but we must not let that spoil the telling of it or mean that we miss the coincidences that just go on happening. If life were not like that we would not believe it. It just happens that Vashti has been banished (1:19) and that Esther, a Jew, takes her place (2:10–17). It just happens that it is Mordecai who overhears the plot to kill the king (2:22) – he was coincidentally in the right place at the right time. It just happens that judgement day (3:7) is eleven months away, therefore there is time for our tale and for deliverance.

Esther, despite being in the right place at the wrong time (5:1), happens to find the king in a good mood. It will also happen that the king cannot sleep, will order his annals to be read (6:1), and the events he hears will be those of 2:21–23 (6:2). It happens that this takes place on the night between Esther's two banquets (5:4; 7:1) and that Haman (Mordecai's sworn enemy, to boot) will be in the court when the king wants to do something for the man he delights to honour (6:6).

I do not need to go on as we have strayed into chapter 6 and the point is made. We have seen coincidence upon coincidence. What good fortune, what luck – what would the chances be of these events all happening? But they do, and they continue to do so. God is not directly interfering; in his sovereign power and goodness he constructs reality and oversees it in such a way that it just so happens that we will all be in the right place at the right time. Paradoxically, of course, in Christ, that place will turn out to be the wrong place – the most wrong place, the gallows intended for Mordecai (5:14–15), the gallows upon which Haman is hanged in Mordecai's place (7:10), the very gallows upon which Jesus hangs in Mordecai's place, Haman's place and in your place and mine.

As Noah (Gen. 6:8), Abraham (Gen. 12:1–3) and a host of others before her (Heb. 11) find favour with God, Esther (5:2–8) finds favour and grace with, in and from King Xerxes. As typologically in her, so too in Christ. We shall be found by that same grace and favour, unexpectedly, undeservedly, on no other basis than that God wills it. It just so happens, fortunately, that God is like King Xerxes. In this one particular respect, the typology of the king is of similarity rather than contrast.

Is it just for the sake of a good story that Esther does not put her request immediately to a seemingly exceptionally receptive king? Is it that Esther knows her king, his vanity, his pride and his self-importance (along with the truth of the proverb that the way to a man's heart is through his stomach)? Does she know that by indulging in flattery, by delaying the satisfaction of his curiosity and by teasing him she will coerce him into giving her what she wants? Is she the archetype of Mary Magdalene at this point or, alternatively, of the blessed virgin? I believe she is neither. As a type of Christ, she is both fully human, shown deploying appropriate wisdom in a highly charged and dangerous adventure, and fully divine, seeking to submit herself, her will and indeed her fate and that of her people to the heart, will and law of the king, as his humble servant and queen. In such submission and service she most truly exemplifies the fullness of both the humanity *and* the divinity of Christ.

In this submissive manner (5:2) she approaches. She says meekly, 'If it pleases the king' (5:4), 'if the king regards me with favour' and 'if it pleases the king' (5:8). She asks the king, together with Haman, to come to another banquet (5:8). She may have been buying herself some time. She may have discerned that now was not yet the right time. She may have calculated that the king, having offered her half of his kingdom twice (5:3,6) and not having had her put to death (4:11) but rather having extended his sceptre and granted her access (5:1), could not then, following two sumptuous banquets, for the sake of his own vanity, pride and glory, refuse her request. She could not have known that later events (chapter 6) would suit her purpose and enable her to find a way for the king to avoid personal implication in the issuing of the first edict – despite the evidence to the contrary (3:10) – and so pin it all on Haman (7:5–6). But that is how it happened. At the end of this fateful day, as the chapter closes, we are no nearer a resolution.

It would not be right to close this particular chapter, however, without turning our attention to Haman. As he encounters Mordecai at the gate again (5:9) he is filled with rage (5:9). He exhibits further character traits as he boasts of 'his vast wealth, his many sons, and all the ways the king had honoured him' above all others (5:11). His pride and vanity, however, find their fullest expression in the satisfaction he takes from the honour paid to him by the double invitation to the table of Queen Esther (5:12). Little does he seem to know that pride goes before destruction (Prov. 16:18). With what presumption does he proceed to have the gallows built for the source of the one blemish on his otherwise clear horizon, Mordecai (5:14)? This presumption, this pride, this plan, will backfire to his own destruction, but for now his self-confidence knows no deflation, save one.

Haman is the completed picture for us of the inexorable development of temptation, sin and death (Jas. 1:14–15) when it has not only the depravity of heart, but the power and the opportunity to act. Let us never forget the depths of our own hearts, as diagnosed by Jesus (Mk. 7:20–23), lest we be too harsh and too judgemental about Haman. Haman is truly every person – we merely lack his power and opportunity. Haman is the betrayer Judas, the deceiver and liar Satan, our father the devil (Jn. 8:44). He is the thief on the cross who rails at Jesus, 'Aren't you the Christ? Save yourself and us!' (Lk. 23:39), he is the rich ruler (Lk. 18:23). It is indeed harder for the first, the powerful, the great, the wealthy and the leaders to enter the kingdom of heaven. Who then can be saved (Lk. 18:26)? The disciples discern rightly that deliverance is impossible for humanity, not just for such a man as Haman, but for all of us. Jesus replies that it is indeed impossible for humanity, yet it is possible for God in and through him. All that is required is that we risk everything (Lk. 18:29), we submit our will to his, and thereby gain access to the throne of grace and receive grace and favour. All that is required she, Esther, the type of Jesus, has accomplished. All we need is to believe it and trust it.

What is necessary is not merely that we be under the sentence of death, the first decree (3:13) or the gallows (7:9), but that in Jesus we already hang on them. All that is necessary to enter the kingdom of heaven is that we indeed lose everything; that we be dead. Fortunately that is the one thing that we all shall be one day. It is the one truly universal fact. Those who are believers now are merely those who have come into a conscious realization that they are truly lost, unclean and dead already. Praise be to God that the consequence of our sin – his judgement and our death in Christ – turns out to be the one thing necessary for our deliverance. This truly is grace. As such, of course, all of us in Haman have the opportunity in death, albeit our last but none the less real chance, to come to our senses and live. You may think I am saying all are delivered. I am. It is not that God won't accept any of us, but that some will not believe and incredibly will refuse his generosity. Some will be the eternal party-poopers.

Let me finish this chapter with this. I do not believe it is coincidental that the drama of this tale of deliverance in Esther focuses in and around a table and a feast (5:4). Like the cycle of the week and the seasons of the year, the table is a focus for our daily family cycle. Jesus recognized this and honoured it while on earth. Again and again he was found at table with sinners, for which he was criticized (Mk. 2:16). Jesus made the party, the feast, the banquet his very watchword for the fullness of the kingdom. Jesus bids us celebrate with ordinary bread and wine the extraordinary deliverance of all humankind made in him in his death. Whether Esther or the writer knew it or not, the president of the telling of the story of God in time and place, the Holy Spirit, knows that it is at the table, in the company of sinners, as often as we eat and drink, that we celebrate the invisible mystery of our deliverance made known in Jesus.

6

Mordecai is Honoured

There are many things I want to include in this chapter, not least because I regard it as the pivot of the drama. Its message of deliverance – the reversal of fortune – is all based upon access to the king. Who will prevail in the inner court of Xerxes – Haman or Esther? Will the evil in the heart of every human being triumph in the face of the wisdom, courage and service of the queen? Will the king, in his pride, vanity and weakness succumb to the wiles of the one or will of the other, or will the kingship with which he is invested finally promote peace, justice and equity for all members of his kingdom?

Before we get to the drama and the answers to these questions, we must set the scene with a brief review of our understanding of kingship. 'That night the king ... ordered ... the record of his reign, to be brought in and read to him' (6:1). What is our first reaction to this? Here is a sad and vain man. Will his greatness and accomplishments bring comfort or induce slumber? Presumably there is no record of any failures, or of things which should have been done by him or by his servants but were not. Paradoxically it is one of the king's failures – to reward Mordecai – that occasions the reversal of Mordecai's fortunes and so significantly serves Esther's purposes and the Jews. Coincidentally, on that night of all nights, the record read to him was the only one that was of crucial importance at this time.

As Xerxes did on that fateful night, we must now briefly turn to the record of the kings of Israel and their execution of the kingship vested in them. We must attempt to put ourselves in a similar position to that of the original readers of the book of Esther and remember the accomplishments and failures of the kings of Israel. We must also remember the conclusions that the biblical writers drew about these records of kingship. Unlike those read to King Xerxes, the conclusions were realistic in their evaluation and assessment. However, I believe it is in this way that they most clearly point to the one who would truly exemplify the nature of kingship as Israel's God intended it. As he 'failed' to fulfil Jewish expectations, 'failed' to establish a kingdom according to their definition, and 'failed' to come down from the Cross, so Jesus succeeded in exemplifying the dependency of the true king who is God's servant.

We shall start our study of the kings of Israel with the book of Judges. Its writer shows their hand when they conclude this book with these words: 'In those days Israel had no king; everyone did as he saw fit' (Judg. 21:25). It appears that the solution to the people's waywardness would be the establishment of a king in Israel, as in other lands. This pointing towards a need for a king seems to me to be a major purpose of the book of Ruth. The final verse of this book, like that of Judges, points forward in hope. Ruth, a foreigner – itself not insignificant in terms of the scope of the (covenant) kingdom – is of the line of 'Jesse the father of David' (Ruth 4:22).

In the books of the prophet Samuel the transition from a charismatic leader, chosen directly as occasion demanded by God for the purpose of the deliverance of his people, to kingship and a unified kingdom is made at the demand of the people (1 Sam. 8:5). With a certain degree of disquiet, as well as a warning of the dangers of a human being being invested with such powers, their request is granted. First Saul (1 Sam. 10:1), then David (1 Sam. 16:12), then Solomon (1 Kgs. 2:12) rule over a unified kingdom in Israel.

A number of points should be made.

- First, in seeking a king it is made clear to the Israelites that they are rejecting Yahweh, an invisible God, in favour of a visible, human symbol as their true king (1 Sam. 8:7; Ps. 47:2–7).

- Second, the experience of partiality, failure, abuse and misdirection with which their history will be littered will be entirely due to the frailty of this visible human symbol and not to God's intended function for kingship in Israel.
- Third, the relationship between God and his people, although now mediated through a king, is in the same covenantal form as it had been for Noah, Abraham, Moses and Joshua.
- Fourth, the covenant promise of blessing a land and many descendants in perpetuity is understood from God's side as unconditional (2 Sam. 7:16), but from the human side is traditionally expressed and understood conditionally: 'If your descendants watch how they live, and if they walk faithfully before me with all their heart and soul, you will never fail to have a man on the throne of Israel' (1 Kgs. 2:4).
- Fifth, the covenant, although it is with the king of Israel, is understood representatively as being through him with Israel and through Israel with all the earth.
- Sixth, this covenant is now vested in the person of the king, who will reign forever in the capital, Jerusalem, where he has built a house for Yahweh – the Temple (1 Kgs. 9:1–9).
- Seventh, the writers' record of this history is highly selective. Seventy-eight out of the 166 chapters that total 1 and 2 Samuel, 1 and 2 Kings and 1 and 2 Chronicles concern David, God's servant, Solomon the son of David and the Temple, the symbol of God's presence in the midst of his people. David, Solomon and the Temple are clearly the focus of history; the exemplars of the writers' view of kingship and kingdom.

A brief survey of this history will clearly demonstrate Israel's failure and that of her kings, as well as the theological and sociological dilemma in which she will be left. Immediately after Solomon's death the kingdom is divided, the northern kingdom of ten tribes being initially ruled by Jeroboam. Jeroboam's name becomes a touchstone for evil in the land: 'So he died, because of the sins he had committed, doing evil in the eyes of the Lord and walking in the ways of Jeroboam and in the sin he had committed and had caused Israel to commit' (1 Kgs. 16:18–19). This verse is the recurring theme and conclusion of the writer upon the northern kingdom, whose people are taken off into exile by Assyria, not to return (2 Kgs. 17:6). The southern kingdom of Judah, two tribes under Rehoboam, does not fare much better. Though there are some better kings, with a far more positive evaluation recorded for us in 2 Chronicles, Judah too is ultimately taken into exile by Babylon (2 Kgs. 25:21).

My son recently volunteered his impression of the Old Testament, having read some of it: 'It's just like *Neighbours* – they're all related to each other.' I think he was implying that they are a mixed bag of ordinary, failing humanity. He had not expected this. I remember my overwhelming disappointment when I first read the whole Old Testament chronologically. I could not find one person who was truly holy, pure, good, triumphant, faithful or successful. I kept hoping that on the next page I would come across just one.

The Old Testament is utterly realistic, heartbreakingly so at times – 'All day long I have held out my hands to an obstinate people' (Is. 65:2; Rom. 10:21). Although there is a partial re-establishment of the covenant purpose of Yahweh with and through his people in the person of Cyrus the Persian (2 Chr. 36:23), and with the rebuilding of the Temple in Jerusalem, this Temple is a pale reflection of its former glory and there is no king. In the words of the prophets the hope of a new form of the covenant remained alive (Jeremiah), as did the hope of a new Exodus (Isaiah), a new Temple (Ezek. 40 – 48) and that in the last days Israel would return and seek their Lord and David their king (Hos. 3:5).

The logic of the biblical historical record demands at least two things:

1 Something and/or someone that is consistent with and fulfils all that has gone before.
2 Something and/or someone that can succeed where all else before have failed.

The other alternative open to the patient God who permits one generation after another to go their own free way has been renounced (Gen. 9:13–16):

> I have set my rainbow in the clouds, and it will be the sign of the covenant between me and the earth … I will remember my covenant between me and you and all living creatures of every kind. Never again will the waters become a flood to destroy all life. Whenever the rainbow appears in the clouds, I will see it and remember the everlasting covenant between God and all living creatures of every kind on the earth.

God has committed himself to working with the raw materials to hand. He will not wipe the slate clean and start all over again.

Before we proceed, let us revisit the seven points made previously regarding kingship in Israel.

- First, despite the rebuilt Temple and puppet king, by the time of Jesus there was a comprehensive feeling that God's voice had long been withdrawn from the land. The withdrawal of God's word was understood as God's withdrawal of himself. The invisible God whom the people had rejected in their demands for a visible king seemed to be absent and deaf to the cries of his people.
- Second, the Hebrew scriptures themselves left the people in no doubt as to their responsibility for God's withdrawal of his word and his hand. Some had remained in exile – Diaspora – but even those who had returned to the Promised Land were a subject people in circumstances not dissimilar from those in Egypt before the time of God's servant Moses.
- Third, the experience of exile had left the people of Israel a changed people, a people of synagogue and book, a fiercely monotheistic people and a people of the covenant.
- Fourth, despite their failure, their responsibility and God's apparent withdrawal, this people clung to God's promised covenant faithfulness and to the prophetic word of a further,

new form of that covenant through which they would be delivered for ever.

- Fifth, this people had lost sight of their representative role and the universal scope of that covenant.
- Sixth, and as a result, the prophetic hope of a covenant in perpetuity between God and his unfaithful people, which was still to be vested in a king such as David reigning in Jerusalem, was wrongly understood in relation to their oppressors, the Romans. This king would be no puppet to the kingdoms of this world and would arise like a star out of Jacob, a sceptre in Israel (Num. 24:17).
- Seventh, the Temple, the symbol of God's dwelling in the midst of his people, would be rebuilt. Access to God would be re-established and God's blessing would be experienced again.

Old covenant visible religion – 'If we ... then God will bless ... but if we do not ... then God will curse...' – will ultimately only result in one thing, cursing. The reality of that curse in the experience of the kingdom of Israel focuses the tension in the heart of God between covenant terms, which inevitably result in cursing, and his love for and compassion towards his people and the impossibility of going back on his elective word to them.

What is the meaning of his unconditional covenant with his people, focused in a king, when that covenant seems permanently broken as one foreign nation after another ruled over Israel?

The historical dominion of the four beasts – Assyria, Babylon, Persia and Rome – was drawing to its close. The promise was that 'one like a son of man ... was given authority, glory and sovereign power ... His dominion is an everlasting dominion that will not pass away, and his kingdom is one that will never be destroyed' (Dan. 7:13–14). The one to come must not only fulfil the word of hope of a new covenant promised by the prophets but must also fulfil the old covenant. He must establish the throne of David and his kingdom around the Temple of God (built by the son of David, Solomon) in Jerusalem forever. The one to come must deliver his people from the judgement they deserve because of their unfaithfulness to the covenant. The one to come must re-establish the access of all to the blessings of God in his kingdom. The one to come will truly be the servant of God, who will serve his people, and in so being he will fully exemplify both God's purpose for the king and the manner of life of those who dwell in his kingdom.

But there is more. The one to come must fulfil the old covenant conditions from the human side. He must be a man of righteousness (Jas. 1:20) and he must succeed where all others before him have so sadly and obviously failed (Mt. 4:1–11). He must also fulfil the demands of a holy God and the consequences of a broken covenant. In gaining access to the throne of God on our behalf, and in making at-one-ment, he must represent not only all Israel, but all humankind.

This one to come, however, will not merely be the priest who approaches God on behalf of his people. At the same time he will also be the sacrifice itself, the means of expiating sin and propitiating its consequences in the heart of God. The one to come will accomplish all this on behalf of all of us so that the ruptures in relationships that we experience with ourselves, with others and with God are truly overcome. All this having been done, he will be seated at the right hand of God as king and priest forever (Heb. 7:17) until that day when all shall see the 'Lion of the tribe of Judah, the Root of David', who is none other than the slain lamb who by his blood has 'purchased men for God from every tribe and language and people and nation' (Rev. 5:5–10).

It is very important to remember that this priest–king has already established his covenant and kingdom forever with all humankind (Heb. 7 – 9) and not just with a selected few on ethnic or religious grounds. History has demonstrated the comprehensive failure of humanity to regain access to the throne of grace. This promised one, the word of promise and fulfilment made flesh, the only qualified representative of all humankind, has, in his own death, mighty resurrection and glorious ascension once and for all been received to the right hand of God. Having pronounced God's verdict at the moment of the accomplishment of all this – 'Father, forgive them' (Lk.23:34) – he awaits, for 'everything is ready. Come to the wedding banquet' (Mt. 22:4).

This one man will thus confirm and fulfil, in a consistent manner, the terms and conditions of the old covenant. He will subject himself to the king for the sake of his people, and gain access to the king in order to make his plea on their behalf. He will receive the grace and favour of the king, and thus the deliverance of the people he represents. In this way he will also succeed where all else before him have failed, including and particularly the representatives of the people: kings and priests. Yet he will not be received by those same people, who will thus make their failure complete. Yet, grace upon grace, he will meet us in the very last place we should or could expect the king to be found, the very worst and lowest place: death. There this king serves us all and raises us all up in his life for the eternal celebration.

I appreciate that this chapter has begun with a long and possibly heavy theological trawl through the history of Israel and its fulfilment, but it is the context for our story and the inheritance of Esther and her people. Jewish readers of this story see it in a particular historical and theological light. Our author hints heavily (6:1) that our reading and their writing of the story will hinge upon our understanding of kingship. For us, as modern readers, that backcloth needs to have been painted in before we proceed. Since we cannot be presumed to be familiar with Israelite history I have taken the liberty of briefly doing that painting.

It seems to me that the story before us immediately lights up. A Persian (Gentile) king in a foreign land, who is ruler of all peoples of every tribe, nation and tongue, is seated on his throne in his capital city, Susa. A certain 'little' people are under the threat of death, through the king's decree. This people are represented by the queen, who has gained the king's initial favour by approaching him, but has yet to make her request known to him. Her people's fortunes still hang in the balance. Will the decree be reversed by the king because of Esther's actions? Will this people be delivered from death? Is God to be found away from Jerusalem? Does God dwell in the midst of his people in a foreign land? Can this land be the land of blessing? Will this blessing be merely upon a certain people or upon all the people in the kingdom? The universal and comprehensive significance of Esther's accomplishment as priest–queen for and on behalf of all people throughout Xerxes' kingdom surely cannot be missed.

The at-one-ment of Xerxes and Esther, male and female, Persian and Jew, king and subject, typologically divine and human, is symbolized no less by Esther's access to the king unsummoned (5:1) than by her intimacy with him when called (4:11). God might desire intimacy, and might desire that with all humankind; he might be approached by a woman; he might not be only located in the Temple in Jerusalem; he might be exemplified by a foreigner; he might permit himself to be the subject of fate; the deliverance of his people might be exemplified by a woman. These ideas have all too often been too much for both Jewish and Christian sensibilities and readership. I do not believe that they are too much for God, nor that they are too far from our writer's mind as they begin this chapter. You must make up your own mind in the light of the evidence.

We know that 'the king could not sleep' (6:1), that the particular portion of the record that was read out recorded Mordecai's part in the conspiracy to assassinate King Xerxes (6:2), and that Haman had just entered the court (6:4). God will accomplish his purpose without recourse to manipulation of people and circumstance. Luck, fate, chance, and accident will be enough. The resolution of the plot, deliverance for the Jews, and its sub-plot, the fate of Haman, do not occur until chapters 7 and 8. Even then there will be a delay until the day they happen (9:1) and are visible. Until then it is to be taken on trust. None the less, I repeat that I believe this chapter to be the hinge upon which all else hangs.

I outlined the structure of the book of Esther in the Introduction. I want to flesh it out slightly here, since we are at what I believe is the turning point of the whole story.

Chapter 3	All honour Haman (3:2)
	First decree of death to the Jews (3:13)
	Xerxes and Haman celebrate (3:15)
	City of Susa is confused (3:15)

Chapter 4	Mordecai approaches Esther (4:5) All Jews fast (4:3,16) Access to the king is planned (4:8,16)
Chapter 5	Esther's first banquet with Haman & Xerxes (5:5) Esther delays her request (5:7–8) Gallows built by Haman for Mordecai (5:14)
Chapter 6	Xerxes determines to honour someone (6:6) Haman honours Mordecai for the king (6:11) Haman's wife foretells Haman's dishonour (6:13)
Chapter 7	Esther's second banquet with Haman and Xerxes (7:1) Esther makes her request (7:3) Haman is hung on the gallows (7:10)
Chapter 8:1–10	Esther obtains premiership for Mordecai (8:2) Access to the king is gained (8:7) Disaster and destruction for the Jews is averted (8:6–9)
Chapter 8:11–17	Mordecai wears the royal robes (8:15) Second decree of life for Jews (8:13) All Jews celebrate (8:17) City of Susa is converted (8:17)

All our themes come together here in a crescendo of anticipation, fulfilment, irony, laughter, reversal and partial relief. We have already noticed the coincidences and accidents. We can almost taste the turnaround in fortune of both Haman and Mordecai: it is comic, tragic and deliciously delightful.

'What should be done for the man the king delights to honour?' (6:6) asks the king, as generous as he is vain, as naïve as he is forgetful, as honourable as he is cruel.

'Who is there that the king would rather honour than me?' (6:6) thinks Haman, as conceited as he is ambitious, as short-sighted as he is vain, as dangerous as he is evil. 'Mordecai the Jew' (6:10), of course.

It is Mordecai who will be the beneficiary of Xerxes' generosity (6:3). This is not because he asked for, worked for, or sought any such reward, nor because he was deserving (3:2) or even because the king was bound to reward him, but because the king was delighted to do so in his freedom and generosity. It is Mordecai who will be publicly honoured (6:9) and who will wear the king's robes (6:11). It is Mordecai for whom fate and ethnicity (6:3), chance (6:2) and the courage (5:1) and wisdom (5:8) of Esther have secured both public honour (6:10) and the predicted reversal of fortune. It is Mordecai who will move from the king's gate and have access to the king's presence (8:15). The undeserving and unlikely Mordecai benefits at the hands of the king through the free combination of circumstances, the malice and evil of Haman and the mediation of Esther. Mordecai is delivered, elevated and raised to a new status and the king delights to honour him. And it is Mordecai who represents us, God's people, all humankind.

In the high court of earth it is Esther who will ultimately gain the decisive access. It is not Haman. All had seemed lost (3:13–15) with Haman very definitely in pole position, elevated higher than all others (3:1). All bowed before him at the king's command (3:2), he ate at the king's table (3:15) and was the possessor of the king's authority (3:10). Yet his conceit, vanity, pride and malice had reached too far both in having the gallows built (5:14) before permission for the execution of the intended victim had been granted (6:4) and in believing himself to be the only object of the king's good pleasure (6:6).

It is this narrowness of vision, this self-conceit, that drove Haman to hate Mordecai and to wish him dead and that ultimately, paradoxically, bring about his own ruin (7:8–10). As Haman's wife Zeresh realizes (6:13), the writing is very definitely on the wall (Dan. 5:5–6). God's sovereign purpose is not for destruction but for deliverance (4:14), and woe betide any who will not conform to the will of the king, and worse, who stands against it. One almost feels sorry for Haman. He is an object of pity and scorn, publicly undressed, mortified, shamed and ultimately suffering the consequences that in his own hatred and malice he had intended for his enemy, Mordecai the Jew (7:10). If it were not for the repetition of the evil intent and evil action of many such as Haman throughout history, one might genuinely feel pity for him. Throughout history circumstances, accident, chance, fate and the courage of many individuals have resulted in the deliverance of the victims of such crimes against humanity as Haman planned. But all too often fortunes have not been reversed, malice and evil have prospered and deliverance has not been forthcoming. Our awareness of that limits our pity. Yet as Haman represents his people, and, just like Mordecai, all humankind, perhaps in pitying him we pity ourselves.

In his sovereign power, purpose and compassion, God demonstrated in this particular instance the reversal of fortune that awaits all on the last day. However, this is no reason for complacency or inactivity, non-co-operation or lack of prayer. Similarly, the fact that in similar historical circumstances God has not always reversed his people's fortunes is no reason for the abandonment of hope or prayer. The signs of his eschatological deliverance of all in and through death, witnessed by those who saw Jesus hanging on the Cross, are his actual deliverances of some here and now. But they are only the signs at which we are right to wonder as we look forward to the reality. The door of hope (Hos. 2:15) is indeed the valley of death.

This chapter is typologically the turning point of all history. It records the events of the night between Esther's two requests, representing the reversal of fortune for all those who can plead nothing but the grace of the king. This reversal is based upon the action of one who dared to approach the king and seek his deliverance and blessing for her people. In the wonder and mystery of God's revelation of the fulfilment of that purpose, it will be in the darkness of the day that separates Good Friday and Easter Sunday, the darkness of the tomb, that the turning point will be. It is the death, resurrection and exultation of

Jesus, to whose activity in the person of Esther we will turn in chapter 7.

Before we do that, however, let us briefly return to where we began this chapter, with the king listening to the record of his reign (6:1). What sort of light does King Xerxes, as a human representation of God, either by way of contrast or by direct parallel, throw upon our understanding of the kingdom of God on earth?

Xerxes is ruler of a kingdom that embraces nations of many cultures and languages (3:14; 8:9). It is a unified kingdom under the one king (1:1). It is a kingdom in which the splendour, glory and majesty of the king is available to the representatives of all peoples (1:3). The king is the descendant of Cyrus and is understood both by the sacred history of Israel (2 Chr. 36:23) and by the religion of the ancients not simply to represent the divine but to be divine. It is a kingdom in which blessing is conditional upon ritualistic sacrifices and appeasement of the divine. It is an everlasting kingdom; the divine faithfulness to covenant promise is intractable. It is a kingdom in which priest as well as king plays an important part in the maintenance of blessing. It is a kingdom in which blessing results from faithful covenant response, and is experienced as deliverance in times of need, and as abundance in times of peace.

In this kingdom justice and equity are not guaranteed for all (3:13), although they are none the less within the gift of the king (8:11). It is a kingdom characterized by foolishness (1:16) not wisdom, weakness (3:10) not strength, failure (3:12) not success, vanity (2:4) not selflessness, fear (4:3) not assurance, doom (3:13) not hope, death (9:5) not life. In this kingdom Yahweh – Israel's covenant-keeping king whose rule extends to all generations and is with all creation – is both exemplified in Xerxes and contrasted with him. This is apparent in the contrast between the exercise of Xerxes' kingship and the fulfilment of true kingship in the form of a servant, as exemplified by Esther.

This universal kingdom is a field in which the word made flesh is comprehensively sown and grows invisibly, bringing forth a mixed response of fruitfulness. This word is not only invisibly at work but paradoxically is the leaven of the whole lump. Its growth is inevitable, but it is accompanied by a parallel development of evil which, for now, God permits and forgives (Mt. 13:30). It is a kingdom characterized by a radical, undeserved, universal and unexpected grace which is equally available to all the labourers in the worldwide vineyard. They are all, whether good or bad, invited to the king's son's wedding banquet. It is a kingdom where all are included, forgiven, loved and accepted unconditionally, but from which some – the powerful, religious, wealthy, those who do not think they need a doctor, and those who will not go into the party with prodigal sons, prostitutes and tax collectors – will exclude themselves. It is a kingdom within which the king and judge will already have pronounced judgement upon himself, and by that means freely vindicated all others.

In this kingdom, the king will humble those who exalt themselves and ask those who are seated lower down to come higher up. The first will be last and the last first. It is a kingdom of reversal in which the lives of those who encounter the king are turned upside down: the blind see, the deaf hear, the lame walk and the dead are raised. It is a kingdom in which the king calls us to follow him and go the way of the Cross, the way of death – to lose everything and so inherit the earth.

This kingdom of God, only a glimpse of which we experience now on earth, is indeed universal, unified, festive, mediated, everlasting, unconditional and blessed. It is just, fair, equitable, secure, guaranteed and open to and for all. Yet its wisdom is apparent foolishness and its strength apparent weakness (1 Cor. 1:18). It is fulfilled as much by Jesus' apparent failure in his death to establish a visible kingdom as it is in its successful fulfilment of all Old Testament types, most particularly in the combination of the roles of priest and king in Jesus, the new Melchizedek (Heb. 5:6). Ultimately – most deeply, most completely and most unexpectedly – the king of Israel, of the nations, of history and of the covenant will typologically be both Xerxes and Esther; not one or the other alone, nor even the two together, but both as one. Kingship will be exemplifed in the suffering obedient service of

Jesus, who demonstrates the fullness of the divine and the human in being king, obedient subject, priest and voluntary sacrifice.

If it is true that Yahweh, as king in Jesus, has already delivered all humankind from everlasting death, then indeed death has lost its sting (1 Cor. 15:55). If this is true, then whether we believe it or not, whether we deserve it or not, whether we co-operate or not, whether circumstances work out or not, whether we are delivered in this life or whether we perish, nothing can separate us from the love of God (Rom. 8:38–39).

This story of a king and queen points us to the gift, the grace and the heart of God, who as king is one with that visible embodiment of kingship, the suffering servant, his son, Jesus. It seems to me that the story is deeply encouraging and potentially liberating. The king of us all has already delivered us all, what-ever may seem to be true. We have a choice: shall we live as if this were true or not? Deliverance is in no sense dependent upon our ability to do anything to, for or in co-operation with him. It has everything to do with the reality that when we needed a king–priest to do what only a king–priest could do, we had one. He was a good one, a faithful one, one in whom we can dare to trust, one who 'did not come to be served, but to serve, and to give his life as a ransom for many' (Mk. 10:45). What do we have to lose by living as if this were true, rather than as if it were not? Why would we live as if we were looking for him rather than as if we had already been found by him? That is more of a mystery to me than the mystery of faith.

7

The Heart of the Story

If chapter 6 was the turning point of this book, then chapter 7 is the heart of the story. For drama, tension, humour, farce, tragedy, caricature, character and courage, these ten verses take some beating. Please read them.

So, as verse 1 tells us, Haman and Xerxes hurried (6:14) to Esther's second banquet (5:8). The content of the story at this point seems to me to be echoed by the tumbling nature – one verse upon another – of the style and pace of this chapter as events move inexorably to their climax.

The king, as on the previous day, is keen to know what Queen Esther wants, not only asking once (5:6) but doing so again: 'What is your petition? ... What is your request?' (7:2). Put Haman and me out of this misery of curiosity! Two banquets, two petitions ... is there to be further prevarication or will the king now be told the reason for these lavish preparations? Isn't it remarkable how motivation always seems to come under scrutiny? A spontaneous gift to your spouse, for example, invites the enquiry, 'So what have you done?' or 'What is this in aid of then? What do you want?' The gift itself will be scrutinized. How much did it cost? How much thought has been given, too much or too little, can very swiftly be misinterpreted, even condemned. Colour, size, cost and timing must all be just right. Esther is treading a very fine line, and a familiar one to many of us.

You will have noticed that Esther has made no impulsive purchase or presentation. All has been very carefully planned, with every attention to detail, so that both men, but particularly King

Xerxes, are put at their ease and made to feel very special.
Perhaps their favourite food has been included in the dinner.
Offering such a treat is only possible in the context of an established relationship. This relationship can be interpreted in
various ways. Esther may be no more than a favourite concubine
from the harem, elevated to the status of queen on the basis of
sexual prowess and physical beauty (2:3,7,17) or lust (J.D.
Levenson, p. 102). But, unless the king is completely self-
absorbed, vain, disloyal and unpredictable – a possibility that the
story itself does not allow us to rule out totally – this seems
unlikely to me. If the king regarded Esther as no more than this,
then the choice with which Esther presents him, between wife
and Prime Minister, is very straightforward.

Alternatively, Esther may be a trusted, intimate wife of much
the same kind that Vashti had been before her. We get a sense of
the king's regard for Vashti in his reaction to her loss once her
fate has been sealed (2:1). He seems – though I admit this may be
reading too much into the text – to miss her and to regret his
actions. He seems to need comfort. In the same way he seems to
be particularly attracted to Esther, as Hegai, the chief eunuch,
had been before him (2:9,17).

It is not beyond our imagination to see Esther as a beautiful
woman, 'lovely in form and features' (2:7) who caught the king's
eye and gave him particular sexual delight (2:16–17). At the
same time she is a woman of such great personal, political and
social sensitivity and charm that the king feels compelled to
answer her request (7:2). She is a queen whom the king recog-
nizes as having great courage, determination and integrity in presenting herself to him, unsummoned and at the risk of death
(5:1), in order to make a request (5:4) on behalf of others.

Esther is not one-dimensional; she grows in favour with all
(2:9,17). The combination of beauty and charm, strength and
submission, wisdom and integrity is remarkable, especially in
contrast to the king's own weakness, prevarication, vanity and
pride, which he may even have recognized himself. It is on the
basis of this relationship, in the context of their intimacy and
with the ground nurtured and prepared, that Esther presents her

request. Is Esther guilty of manipulation? Does the selfless end, representation of the cause of her people, justify the means? I feel that Esther deports herself in such a way that the king, while he may seem to be led by the nose, is in reality led gently and lovingly to a good place to which he would want to go and to which he would be grateful to be led without any loss of male, royal face. I believe that means and ends should be consistent. I do not find malice, underhandedness or manipulation in Esther's dealings with the king. I have two reasons for this. First, I probably am to a large extent a romantic. I do not want to see anything worse than pragmatism in my heroine and want to give her the benefit of any doubt. You may, of course, feel differently, identifying rather with other characters in this story with whom I have dealt less sympathetically. Second – and I'm not sure whether this is more or less significant – Esther, as the type of Jesus, could not think, speak or act in any way other than in accordance with the king's will, or with her place in the king's heart. Jesus, of course, does not grow in any less wisdom or fortune than Esther, nor does he act with any less practical wisdom than she. Perhaps it is possible and acceptable to be both romantic and practical, typological and developmental.

   You may by now feel frustrated that I am not getting on with the story. The delay has been intentional. God's interaction with his world, history and us as individuals is recorded for us in the form of story and still occurs in that form. There are always a number of possible outcomes. We always have freedom of choice. Accidents do happen. Strokes of luck – unexpected or unwelcome as they often are – over which we have no control do occur. We can respond to them and take responsibility. Our lives, Esther's life and the details of the journey are not pre-ordained or already mapped out. There is genuine risk, anxiety and excitement. Has it ever occurred to you that it took Jesus three years to journey from Nazareth to Jerusalem? That says to me that he was at least as interested in the journey and the relationships along the way as he was in the destination. What, finally, is the answer to the questions 'Where is this world, this government, this football team, your marriage, my life, going?' The answer is into the universal drainpipe of history, the dread statistic, the one place that many dare not speak about, yet most fear and all know awaits – death. So if everything will be lost, if everyone will die, what more can we possibly have to lose upon the way? Why should we not take the time to journey in trust, to take a risk or two, to see what there is to see, become whatever we become? We may fail, look silly, be rejected – everything may go wrong. If we know that everything will end anyway, and that in and through the worst that can happen, death, God will bring deliverance and life, why not hazard a little, or even a lot? That is what Esther does.

At the beginning of the chapter, Esther knows at least that she has found favour with the king (5:2). She has not been executed (4:11), and has both put the king in a good mood (5:6) and made him curious by further delaying her petition (5:8) until the following day (7:2). Now is the time. Xerxes has the power of life and death. Will Esther find the king – despite their relationship, despite her tactics, despite the circumstances and the propitiousness of the moment – determined to side with his male Prime Minister, Haman? Will the king decide against Esther's request, either because he delights in Haman more (3:1,10) or because his decree is irreversible (1:19) and there is nothing even he can do? Or will he decide in her favour? The situation may indeed prove hopeless and deliverance may be impossible. We also know, even if Esther may not, that the sub-plot of Haman's relationship with Mordecai is approaching its climax. Who will hang on the gallows?

Esther is in the delicate position of having presented this absolute ruler of all the earth with a dilemma. Will he be angry that she has deceived him about her ethnicity? Will he be angry with her for presenting him with yet another difficult decision (1:15; 2:4; 3:11) which he is ill equipped to make and for which he needs another's advice (7:9)? Or, far worse, will King Xerxes be angry with Esther for reminding him of the edict spelling doom for a 'certain people' (3:8) – who turn out to include his wife – for which he is ultimately responsible? The situation could not be more delicate. However propitious the circumstances, however secure her relationship with him, however just the cause, these considerations at times seem almost irrelevant in this kingdom. Can Esther deliver her people, Mordecai and herself without embarrassing the king? At the same time, can she defeat the evil and the far more politically-astute Haman?

I want to tell you a story.

> There were two men in a certain town, one rich and the other poor. The rich man had a very large number of sheep and cattle, but the poor man had nothing except one little ewe lamb that he had bought. He raised it, and it grew up with him and his children. It shared his food, drank from his cup and even slept in his arms. It was like a daughter to him.
>
> Now a traveller came to the rich man, but the rich man refrained from taking one of his own sheep or cattle to prepare a meal for the traveller. Instead he took the ewe lamb that belonged to the poor man.
>
> When King David heard this he burned with anger against the man and said, 'As surely as the Lord lives, the man who did this deserves to die! He must pay for that lamb four times over, because he did such a thing and had no pity.'
>
> Nathan the prophet said to King David, 'You are the man!'

This story can be found in 2 Samuel 12. I wanted to tell it in full partly because it is so delightful and partly because it points us back once again to the person, character, heart and work of the king of Israel in relationship to his people and his God. But I wanted to tell it mostly because it seems to me that our writer is alluding to it in the way they record Esther's method of encountering David's equivalent, King Xerxes.

Like Nathan the prophet before her, Esther contrives a way to bring the force of her position home to the king with the most impact. 'If I have found favour … if it pleases your majesty, grant me my life' (7:3). She continues deliciously, delicately, enticingly to withhold information until its full force might be felt. The drama could not be greater. I am convinced that where I have stopped the above quotation there is a pause. The king is in shock. What? Who would dare threaten the life of my queen? Esther continues, 'If we had merely been sold as male and female slaves, I would have kept quiet, because no such distress would justify disturbing the king' (7:4). Mere slavery would not have been enough, but this is life and death. Notice that she has slipped her Jewish identity into the story – she says 'we'. The king was both curious to know what Esther's request would be and desperate to answer it (5:6; 7:2). Now he is absolutely furious (7:7,10), as he had been once before (1:12).

So, like King David before him, King Xerxes demands to know, 'Who is this man? Where is he?' In our story, however, Esther points the finger away from the king, who we presume would know little of the repentance that overtook King David, or indeed that experienced by Haman, for whom, were it not for the fact that he is such a proud, vain, evil man, we might at this point be feeling very sorry. Esther reports that the one responsible is none other than Haman, who is at dinner with them (7:6).

Haman is understandably terrified (7:6). The king, as decisive as ever, runs out into the garden (7:7). What will he do? I imagine that he is not only furious, but now confused, totally unable to think for himself yet compelled to respond to Esther's request. This is not because of the injustice done to Esther's people, whom she represents, but because his person and his pride have been affronted and his possession, Esther, has been threatened. Esther, the Jews and the world await.

With some delightful irony our author contrives to resolve the difficulties of the king. Haman falls (7:8) on Esther's couch. Mordecai would not fall (3:2), the lot had fallen (3:7), and Zeresh predicted Haman would fall (6:13), thus confirming his own downfall (7:8). This confirms the elevation of Mordecai, Haman's sworn enemy (8:2), in his place, the reversal of his evil decree (9:1) and deliverance for the Jews. The whole tale had been precipitated by Haman's correct interpretation of Mordecai's refusal to fall before him, while his fate (7:7) is sealed through Xerxes' misinterpretation of the same act (7:8). Such is the pattern and order of reversal in this world – beware lest ye fall!

Fortunately for the king – whom our author consistently presents as being incorrigibly indecisive and utterly unable to think for himself – one of his eunuchs, Harbona, happens to be present at that moment (7:9). A gallows happens to be available and so the death penalty upon Haman can be carried out immediately (7:10). In a later chapter we will look at the question of the death penalty in greater depth. For now let us note that we feel justice seems to demand the death penalty in this case because of Haman's evil intentions and actions against an entire people, the Jews. Perhaps for molesting the queen something less stringent might have been more appropriate. From Esther's point of view, while the sub-plot may have been resolved, the major item on her agenda is still outstanding. This will be the subject matter of the next chapter. From the king's point of view, despite the need for a new Prime Minister, which itself will serve Esther's purpose, the matter is closed. His honour is upheld, he has sustained no loss of face – a matter of not inconsiderable importance to a king, nor any man – the affront has been removed and his 'fury subsided' (7:10).

I think it is perhaps a pity that Esther did not appear to Jesus on that mountain (Lk. 9:30–31) as well as, or in place of, Moses and Elijah. It might once and for all have guaranteed the equality of man and woman in the kingdom and removed the theological ground for gender and ethnic abuse in church history. As it is, a woman did not appear to Jesus at the turning point in his ministry, and the rest is history.

You may have noticed a sharp change in direction. Just in case your attention has lapsed and you have missed it, let me make the connection. Esther does not only act as priest–mediator between God and her people in daring to approach the king (5:1), she does not only additionally put on royalty (5:1) and approach the king in her capacity as queen, but she also fulfils typologically the third office of the Christ to come in walking in the footsteps not merely of Nathan the prophet, but also of Moses the prophet (Deut. 18:18). It is in their capacity as prophetic forerunners that Moses and Elijah appear with Jesus (Mk. 9:4). It seems to me that Esther cannot appear in that way typologically because she is not a forerunner like Moses and Elijah. Rather, she stands alongside Joshua and Elisha. Moses is denied access to the Promised Land; Joshua is granted it. Moses fails to lead the Israelites into the Promised Land; Joshua succeeds. Moses fails to fulfil the promised deliverance; Joshua completes the task. Likewise, Elijah returns to the place of old covenant revelation, Mount Sinai; Elisha inherits a double portion. Elijah experiences royal disapproval and stands alone; Elisha speaks on behalf of Israel, the king and on the stage of world history, demonstrating that Yahweh is indeed Elohim. Elijah brings the widow's son back to life; Elisha is archetypally the prophet of the resurrection.

Whereas Moses' name means 'drawn out of the water' (Ex. 2:10) (an allusion to baptism) and Elijah's name means 'Yahweh is my God', Joshua's name means 'saviour', and Elisha's 'God is my salvation'. Esther, who will arise to deliver her people, typologically stands with Joshua and Elisha and hence could not stand with Jesus on the mount of transfiguration. Moses and Elijah, being types of the forerunner (cf. John the Baptist), do stand with Jesus to talk of the deliverance he will accomplish in Jerusalem through his death. I appreciate that the types are not clear-cut. Moses does lead his people out in the Exodus, as Jesus will, and Elijah does ascend to heaven, as Jesus will, but I believe that at this point Esther is even greater than Moses and Elijah in the sense of filling out and fulfilling the work of their illustrious forebears. She is more like Joshua and Elisha than Moses and Elijah.

I now want to demonstrate a partial contradiction of the above in order to underline further the point that the typology is not clear-cut. While I believe that Esther fulfils the prophetic hope and accomplishes the deliverance of her people, at the same time she also stands as a prophetess in her own right. Our author alludes, I believe, to her function as a prophet, like Moses. I do not think it is for mere effect, as discussed above, that in approaching Xerxes – as Moses approached the Pharoah many years before her – Esther alludes to the slavery of her people (Ex. 1:11). Deliverance from slavery is understood not only sociologically but theologically, from the slavery of law and sin

(Gal. 3 – 4). Moses obtained the deliverance of his people not merely from slavery – which, though painful, is only temporal – but also from its logical consequence, death. In Egypt the Israelites escaped the wrath of the Pharoah and the angel of death through the blood of the young rams and goats (Ex. 12:13). Esther likewise seeks the deliverance of her people from the king's decree of death (3:12). Furthermore, as Moses sought for the presence, protection, guidance and blessing of Yahweh to be with the Israelites as they journeyed, on the basis of his special favour with him (Ex. 33:12–14), so Esther, as J.D. Levenson says, is 'the sovereign's darling' (p. 101).

Like Moses before her, therefore, Esther seeks the special favour and blessing of the king so that her people might be delivered from slavery and death. In contrast to Moses, however, the deliverance she sought for her people is experienced in the land of exile. Whereas Moses failed to reach the Promised Land of blessing and remained in the wilderness, Esther experiences blessing paradoxically and remarkably in the land of exile. That Esther is so closely paralleled to Moses, and indeed in some respects shown to be greater than he, and that the deliverance she accomplishes results in the blessing of God's people in a foreign land, leads me to conclude that accommodation is at least an acceptable way for the people of God to live in a foreign culture. The fact that God does not intervene miraculously to accomplish the deliverance of his people is to me another indication that sacred dress, religious language, separatist behaviour and answered prayer are not at the core of the faith of the faithful. The grand metanarrative of all history is deliverance. It appears that this deliverance, or reversal in fortune, can be sought and accomplished without any intervention on the part of Yahweh. Perhaps his not performing one is the greatest miracle of all.

I am fully aware that some may regard this typological form of interpretation as somewhat fanciful, but without it it seems to me that the story of Esther becomes merely one of God's deliverance of his people through providence rather than miracles. However delightfully it is told, this is a limited message and it does not deserve the kind of attention I am giving it. In order to

demonstrate further that my interpretative key is not as fanciful
as it may appear, I want, before closing this chapter, to look at the
calendar for our story.

On the 'same day' (8:1) as the events of our chapter the
counter-edict for the deliverance of the Jews is sought and then
issued (8:9). But what day is this? The night before 'the king
could not sleep' (6:1). The day before, when Esther had 'put on
her royal robes and stood in the inner court of the palace' (5:1),
unsummoned, was the third day of the Jewish fast (4:16), itself
the result of Esther hearing from Mordecai (4:8) of the king's
edict of genocide 'to destroy, kill and annihilate all the Jews –
young and old, women and little children – on a single day, the
thirteenth day of the twelfth month, the month of Adar' (3:13).
This third day of the fast is the first day on which Esther's plan is
enacted. The second day (7:1) sees that plan's success and the
third day (which will turn out to be the seventieth [8:9] and
which we shall explore in the next chapter) sees its irreversible
accomplishment (8:11). The counter-decree, the Jewish deliverance that resulted and the celebrations that ensued in the twelfth
month (3:7; 9:1) were all the direct result of the issue of the first
decree following the casting of the lot on the thirteenth day of the
first month (3:12).

These are all very specific time markers which to a Jewish
reader will have great significance, but to us seem meaningless
and therefore are easily lost. It just so happens that the date of the
issue of the first decree is one day before Passover (Lev. 23:5–6).
The date of the programme for the destruction of the Jews itself
is one day before Purim, which would be celebrated in perpetuity
in addition to the Levitical feasts in memory of Esther. This link
is either just another one of those things that happened, in
history or in the mind of our author, or is entirely intentional and
may be seen by those who have eyes to see. I believe we are meant
to see links between Moses and Esther, Passover and Purim, and
Esther and Jesus.

To repeat, through the miracle of non-intervention God will
accomplish his purpose of deliverance, whether we say we
believe in him, seek it, give thanks to him, see his hand at work or

not. By some means, relief and deliverance for God's people will arise (4:14), whether we actively co-operate, are silent, are passive or not. What a relief this is. God is not dependent upon us. What a liberation – we are free to respond as we wish, and rather than out of guilt or duty. We need have no sense that if we get it wrong, or deviate from the path, we may be lost forever, for we are lost and we will consistently get lost again and again (Lk. 15). Yet having found us he will bring us home rejoicing. He is faithful and dependable, he is there, he has always been there and will always be there with us. If we perish, we perish (4:16) and yet he is there. The counter-edict is issued, God's banner over us is love (Song 2:4). Believe it or not, it is true.

Finally in this chapter I want to refer back to something I raised earlier, only to say that I will deal with its resolution – or rather its being held together in tension – more fully later. It is this. The responsibility for the plight of the Jews (representing humankind) is not Haman's (typologically every person), but Xerxes the sovereign lord's (typologically Yahweh). It is his ring (3:10) that is used, albeit in a delegated capacity, to seal the genocidal edict. Esther, the type of prophet, king and priest, will seek the deliverance of her people from the decree of death sealed by the hand of King Xerxes. In the end the responsibility for the events of history and our individual lives results from the freedom that God gives us (Gen. 3:11–13).

While the story of deliverance may be wearing particular cultural and historical clothes in the book of Esther, it is our story, the story of all of us. We are delivered and God has provided for that deliverance typologically in the person of Esther and in the person of Jesus. But more than that, deeper still, the story is concerned not merely with the at-one-ment of God and humankind, nor merely the at-one-ment of humankind within ourselves and with one another, but with the at-one-ment within God himself. How can he deliver himself from acting most justly upon the wrath and indignation within himself, evidenced in the first decree of genocide? We will see in the counter-decree the grace, compassion and mercy of God towards his people. For a clearer vision still, we must wait for the revelation of Jesus, for in Jesus is the most complete at-one-ment. The first decree will take its full effect not in justly sentencing, condemning and executing humankind, but in its reversal in the sentencing, condemnation and execution of Jesus, the judge, in our place. The second decree will become fully manifest in his resurrection and exultation to the right hand of God. Through him our fortunes are totally reversed and our deliverance complete. It is this dilemma in the heart of God, built into the conclusion of our story in chapter 8, to which we must now turn.

The Terminus

If chapter 6 was the turning point in the writer's chiastic structure for the book of Esther and chapter 7 the book's dramatic core, then this chapter is the terminus to which it has been heading.

On the first day, recorded for us as the third day of Esther's fast (4:16; 5:1), Esther approached King Xerxes. She asked him to come to dinner with her the next day and to bring Haman (5:4). That night (6:1) King Xerxes could not sleep, the records of his rule were consulted and, on the next day – the second day – Haman was required to reward and honour Mordecai the Jew, his sworn enemy, for whom he has had a gallows built. On the evening of the second day (7:2), Haman and Xerxes dine with Esther again. Haman's downfall leads to the king's anger subsiding (7:10) and the promotion of Mordecai (8:2) in Haman's place to the office of Prime Minister.

Mordecai, who had forbidden Esther to reveal her ethnic and family background when being taken to the king's harem (2:10), is rewarded with the office of Prime Minister as a direct result of Esther's ignoring his command about not revealing her ethnicity (7:3) and kinship to Mordecai (8:1) to King Xerxes. It is thus not only Haman but also Mordecai who is the object of the writer's deep irony. This is further amplified when Esther appoints Mordecai over Haman's estate (8:2). It seems clear to me that her initial subordination and dependency has been decisively reversed. However, I think we shall see in Esther a more sensitive, delicate and equitable handling of their new and relative status as the story is rounded off in chapters 9 and 10. Esther is now not only queen in title (2:17), but is acting as such as an exemplar.

Let us now return to our writer's chronology. With such a tight time frame between the issue of the first edict on day thirteen of the first month (3:12), and Queen Esther's request (8:3–6) on the second day after her three-day fast following its proclamation, I find it surprising that the second equal and opposing edict should be published on the twenty-third day of the third month (8:9). Why the delay? Wouldn't it be more likely that this edict would be published the next day, i.e. the third day? Of course, from the time of publication and performance of the second edict there are still a full nine months to the day on which it came to force in the twelfth month, the month of Adar (3:13; 9:1). It could be argued that there is no real urgency. However, in view of the writer's obvious care over dating, I cannot help but look for a further and deeper significance for this delay.

We have already had cause to look at the writer's use of the number seven, a biblical number of universal application and appreciation denoting completeness. The introductory chapters of the book record events that took place in the first seven years of King Xerxes' reign, concluding with Esther's coronation as queen (2:16) in the seventh year. We will find that the feast of Purim, established as a result of the Jewish deliverance, will be celebrated in every generation, by every family, in every province and in every city throughout all generations (9:28). So the opening epoch of King Xerxes' reign, recorded in chapters 1 and 2 and characterized by celebration, is mirrored by the celebrations in perpetuity that have resulted from the execution of his two edicts. The descriptions of these parallel events effectively bracket the drama of chapters 3 – 8. That drama is conducted within a framework of two sets of three days, the exchanging of sackcloth and ashes for royal garments (4:1; 8:15), fasting turning to joy (4:3; 8:16) and confusion becoming conversion (3:15; 8:17).

While it seems likely to me that this chronology is a direct result of history, its presentation is very stylized and is deliberately set within a chiastic doublet structure in order to emphasize the pattern of reversal that the author sees and wishes to draw to our attention. We cannot miss the numerology or the chronology. I am grateful to J.D. Levenson (p. 110) for making the connection for me that between the date of the issue of the first and second edicts there are two months and ten days – that is seventy (or possibly seventy-two) days. The number seventy, as we have already seen, would have had a deep resonance for Esther's Jewish readership as the number of years of the exile (Jer. 29:10). But we can go further. The members of Jacob's family who went to Egypt were seventy in all (Gen. 46:27), the number of the Israelites' eldership under Moses was seventy (Ex. 24:1) and the Israelites' anticipated life span recorded in the prayer of Moses is also seventy years (Ps. 90:10). Just as with the number seven, there is symbolism of completeness, universality and of representation in the number seventy. The Jews in exile no less than the returnees in Judea could celebrate the end of their exile. In the seventy elders all Israel is represented, and after seventy years all Israel is delivered. So it is that after seventy days the second edict of life for the people of God – as opposed to the first edict of death – is issued.

But we can go further still, I believe (though this may be too fanciful for some) and see in Jesus' dispatch of the seventy, interpreted as seventy-two in the New International Version (Lk. 10:1–17), a similar symbolic understanding of this number, either in the mind of Luke or Jesus or both. Jesus has already sent out the twelve (Lk. 9:1–2). He then sends out the seventy, confirming, as I see it, the universality and the comprehensiveness of the gospel of deliverance. This deliverance is not merely for Israel, or even for all exiles, but for all the world, linked as his commission is with the story of the Good Samaritan (Lk. 10:25–37). This complete deliverance of all, ultimately revealed in and through Jesus' word and work as forgiveness of sins, is pronounced not once, nor merely seven times, but seventy times seven (Mt. 18:21–22). This is indeed a complete, comprehensive universal deliverance that is for everyone, forever and everywhere. Forgiveness is God's last word on our sin.

If that is insufficiently fanciful for your taste, we can, I believe, explore still further. 'Today, if you hear his voice, do not harden your hearts' says the writer to the Hebrew Christians (Heb. 3:15; 4:7), quoting their scriptures (Ps. 95:7–8) to them in a present and urgent manner as though they were the very words of God today to them and to us – which is, of course, what he believed them to be (Heb. 3:7), as indeed do I. 'Encourage one another daily, as long as it is called Today' (Heb. 3:13). 'And on the seventh day God rested from all his work ... [but] they shall never enter my rest' (Heb. 4:4–5). 'Therefore God again set a certain day, calling it Today ... a Sabbath-rest for the people of God' (Heb. 4:7–9). For anyone who has believed has entered that rest (Heb. 4:3) which Israel had not entered into because of their disobedience (Hebrews 4:6). 'For if Joshua had given them that rest [in the Promised Land – and likewise returning exiles genera-tions later] God would not have spoken later about another day' (Heb. 4:8).

It is this other day, this third or seventieth day, to which I believe our writer is pointing typologically. The writer to the Hebrews clearly believed that this day is not a twenty-four hour period, but the age in which those first Christians were living and in which we now live. Presumably this was on the basis that Jesus is the same yesterday, today and forever (Heb. 13:8). Esther, the typologically prophetic word of God, lives and is active (Heb. 4:12), at least in this particular sense, today. Esther, typologically the priest–king forever in the order of Melchizedek (Heb. 5:6), offers us a complete, comprehensive and universal word and work. Having entered typologically into the Holy of Holies and made purification for sins of the whole world, once and for all, she has 'sat down at the right hand of the Majesty in heaven' (Heb. 1:3).

Jesus has entered the Sabbath rest of God and, his work com-plete, he has sat down. All is accomplished, for all and forever. There can be no more to do; everything has been done. Every-thing has been prepared for the feast to begin – indeed, it has already begun. As God rested after the work of creation, so Jesus rests after the work of the new creation. As all humankind, in Adam and Eve, enjoy the blessings of God's work in the garden, so have all humankind entered into the eternal banquet in Jesus Christ, the second Adam. I do not want this point to be lost, but I am not unaware that you will be wondering how this Sabbath rest of God, this eternal party for all accomplished in and through Jesus, may be entered into by faith. Nor am I unaware that you will be wondering how this eternally established reality may be experienced not only in the eternal today of God but in our today in this age. We shall return to the question of trust and faith later. But let us have no doubt that in Jesus we have a great high priest who has entered the inner court of the king, who has made the one perfect sacrifice (Heb. 10:10) and who has accomplished the universal deliverance of Israel, non-returning exiles, Samaritans and Gentiles. Jesus fills out and fills up Esther's determination to hazard her own life (4:16).

But let us go further still. Now the reader may decide we are definitely too fanciful! Our writer, under the presidency of the Holy Spirit, reveals not merely that God is a God of deliverance through reversal; that he accomplishes his purposes with or without our co-operation (4:14); that he accomplishes that purpose with (Israel's sacred history) or without (Israel's secular history in microcosm as recorded in Esther) miraculous intervention; or that that deliverance and forgiveness is all embracing, of all and for always. They reveal that this gospel is available, true and accessible now.

On the third day of the fast, Esther puts 'on royal robes' (5:1) to intercede and to make peace between Xerxes and her people. On the third day, which, it turns out, is the seventieth day (8:9), the equal and opposite counter-decree of life is drawn up. On the third day the Sabbath rest of God began in the resurrection of Jesus and, while it will be entered into on the last day, it may be entered into today. You may be feeling a sense of confusion about which day is today. I hope that it is not simply because of my presentation of the material. As Jesus is the same yesterday, today and forever, and his deliverance took three days, 'today' is characterized by all three days. Today is always the first day, when, in

Esther, life is hazarded and, in Jesus, given up. Today is always the second day, the Sabbath, Saturday, when in the mystery and heart of God the Father, Son and Holy Spirit the mediation of the death of Jesus is offered and accepted. Today is always the third day, the resurrection Sunday, the seventieth day, the seventy times seven day of the proclamation of forgiveness and life available to everyone, always.

Today is always therefore Good Friday, Sabbath Saturday and Resurrection Sunday. All of history is squeezed into and out of those three days, recorded for us in the narrative of the book of Esther. Whether our author like Abraham before them rejoiced at the thought of seeing Jesus' day (Jn. 8:56) we can only guess. I hazard and hope that they did, maybe not in the clarity of the gospel narrative but perhaps through an even darker glass darkly (1 Cor. 13:12). So today, if you hear his voice, do not harden your heart to Jesus who will always hazard his life, mediate on our behalf and thankfully be favourably received by God.

This brings us to the incompleteness of the sight of our author as well as a further aspect of the depth of their insight into the world, experience and circumstance of the Jews in Persia, and indeed all humankind. As we have seen, our author places emphasis on twos. The fullness of the biblical revelation of the three or the third is only hinted at. Furthermore, in the two edicts that mirror one another (3:12–15; 8:9–14) we have an edict of death and an edict of life expressing the reality in which we all find ourselves. I hope I do not have to demonstrate the truth of this statement. Surely it is self-evident that all of us experience both blessing and cursing, joy and suffering, health and sickness, life and death? Will we experience life again from death? If so, how? Again, our writer points to this truth through the providential deliverance of a powerless minority in the story. In the same way the more sacred writers before them have pointed to the same deliverance through the miraculous intervention of God. The fullness of the revelation of the non-interventionist, providential deliverance accomplished by God in the death of Christ must wait for the fullness of the New Testament story and revelation. We approach, in my view, the very heart of this story in Esther – the very heart of the gospel and indeed the very heart of God.

How can the two edicts be reconciled? Must they be held in tension? Which will triumph ultimately? It is my conviction that the solution to this will be revealed fully in the story of Jesus, but that the manner of its resolution is hinted at by our author in 8:13. We will look in the next chapter at the issues of the death penalty, killing, murder, holy war and the like. I want for the time being to concentrate on one word: 'avenge'.

I was put on to this by M.V. Fox (p. 101), who takes issue with George E. Mendenhall's translation of the word usually appearing as 'avenge' as 'vindicate' in his work *The Tenth Generation: The Origins of the Biblical Tradition* (Baltimore, MD: Johns Hopkins University Press, 1973). M.V. Fox takes the view that 'avenge' is a more appropriate translation. He then seems to contradict himself by concluding that though the Jews could have, and perhaps should have, they did not 'actually execute blood vengeance but rather exercise force whose legitimacy derives from the king' (M.V. Fox, p. 101). On the one hand he seems not to accept the possible translation 'vindicate', and yet on the other hand does not want to take the full force of the word 'vengeance' but waters down the translation to 'necessary, legitimate force exercised in one's self-defence with the authority of the king'. While I believe this was the case – and we will explore this further in the next chapter – I want to retain both translation options in their full weight.

Again, whether the Hebrew will allow it (I am certainly no Hebrew scholar, but take it that a debate between those who are suggests there are alternatives), the theology demands, it seems to me, a more fluid, heavier and ultimately irreconcilable tension in the word which may equally well be translated 'avenge' as 'vindicate'. Both are heavyweight words. On that day, would the Jews avenge themselves? Would they be avenged? Would they vindicate themselves? Would they be vindicated? The ambiguity of translation seems to me to point to the equal and opposite sides of the writer's view of the world, expressed in the two edicts. Will the Jews die or live? Will they be delivered or not? Will the first decree of genocide, issued the day before Passover, result in vengeance or vindication? And for whom? Will the second decree of life, taken up the day before Purim, be celebrated in perpetuity? Will the people of God always live with and in the tension of the two edicts, as history might indicate, or will there be a glorious at-one-ment of the two which may in some way be anticipated by the people of God and participated in today?

Once again, the moment I express the problem like this, it becomes clear to me that our writer is typologically directing our attention through Esther to Jesus. Furthermore the Holy Spirit, yet more wonderfully still, is revealing to us that this glorious deliverance, this radical change in fortunes and this reversal for the people of God from death to life, is accomplished in Jesus, who is both the object of God's vengeance and the means of God's vindication. It is ultimately not through death but out the other side of it that life is experienced. The ultimate, wonderful, glorious, mysterious accomplishment of the deliverance of the people of God is accomplished as Haman's genocidal edict of death is entered into by Jesus, as his life is emptied out, as his cup is filled up and as the will of Haman (Satan) is shown to be none other than the will of Xerxes (God) after all.

This is the ultimate reversal, the ultimate turning of the tables (9:1), the at-one-ment of the two edicts. Jesus is both the man of righteousness who can offer himself as a faithful covenant partner, responding in love and obedience and as a once and for all sacrifice. Yet as he is also the man of sin so identified with us, yet without sin, he can take upon himself the wrath of God on Good Friday. He waits on the Sabbath Saturday and then is raised up on Easter Sunday, forever gloriously scarred, forever the at-one-ment for all. This is the object of our faith, this is the word of hope, this is the one whom we gratefully love.

A glance at Deuteronomy 32:35–36 reveals, I suggest, how vengeance and vindication may be viewed as one: 'It is mine to avenge ... The Lord will vindicate [my translation] his people.' Under the terms of the covenant the unfaithful covenant partner, God's people, would deservedly experience God's curse. (As I understand this form of the covenant to be an expression of the covenant God made with all creation in Noah [Gen. 9:8–11], God's covenant partner Israel represents all humankind.) Yet God, the faithful covenant partner, will not let go of his people, however unfaithful, and will maintain the honour of his name and the terms of his covenant because of his unfailing love for his people – all people.

We live under both the covenant curse, the edict of death, and the covenant blessing, the edict of life. This is the common lot of all humanity. Our common lot is not an either/or reality, but a both/and reality. Deliverance is not necessarily experienced now as relief from the first edict, though sometimes, for some, as for the Jews in the time of Esther, thankfully that is the case. In the same way, the non-deliverance from the curse experienced every bit as much by those with faith as those without is not the full story. This is exemplified by the Jews of twentieth-century Europe. The ultimate deliverance is not an escape from the first edict into the land of the second edict, but an at-one-ment of both, glimpsed today but only fully manifest on the last day on the other side of death.

Our reality today is a three-day reality (Good Friday, Sabbath Saturday and Easter Sunday), experienced in time on earth this side of our participation in the means of access, this side of our entrance through the gateways to its at-one-ment in our own deaths. Whether the suffering that is experienced is undeserved or the deserved consequence of sin, the first edict of death comes to all. Satan's words, 'You will not surely die' (Gen. 3:4) are shown to be what they are, a lie. We will die. We experience and must experience the full measure of God's vengeance and judgement. Yet God wants us to live that we should be delivered, that we should be vindicated. God's covenant word to Adam, Noah, the patriarchs and David cannot fail. God must be faithful and his name must be honoured. God's 'no' must be God's 'yes'. Satan's lie must be God's truth. Satan's will that all must die is fulfilled in Jesus' submission to him on the Cross, yet, at the same time, it turns out that this is God's will.

God's judgement has fallen upon Jesus and through him on all humankind. God's vindication of Jesus to resurrection and life is, likewise, his final verdict upon all humankind. So it comes about that Satan's will is God's will and Satan's word is God's word: 'You will not surely die.' Believe it or not, it is true. At the cost of his own life, Jesus makes the at-one-ment of the two edicts. In Jesus we are all condemned and all justified. In the judgement pronounced and executed upon Jesus we, the accused, are acquitted and the judge judged.

We glimpse this partially in our story, as in chapter 9 the Jews participate in their own deliverance by co-operating with God and defending themselves from their enemies. How we live today in the light of the tension and at-one-ment of the two edicts will be the subject matter of the next chapter. Let us complete this one by gazing in wonder, adoration and praise at him to whom our text points as the fulfilment of the mediation and intercession of Queen Esther.

Unlike those Jews in Esther's day, we have no participation in or co-operation with God, who in Jesus has done everything necessary for our eternal deliverance. We merely receive the free and complete vindication and leave the vengeance and judgement to God, who in Jesus has drunk that cup to the very dregs. That is why Jesus (Mt. 7:1) and his brother James (Jas. 4:11–12) are so strong in their warnings against judging others. To judge others is to fail to see that in so doing we are self-condemned. To judge others is to fail to see that I am as equally and rightly condemned as my brother or neighbour. To judge others is to demonstrate our ignorance of the end to judgement in Jesus. To judge others is to fail to realize that the judgement has been passed on me, my brother and my neighbour in Jesus and we have all been acquitted – we may all walk out free. To judge others is to deny this verdict and to take to ourselves the judgement that has already been passed on him. To judge others is to fail to realize that God's judgement of our determination to judge has already been fulfilled in Jesus. This is blessed resistance indeed to our demand for the right to sit in judgement, that we might be vindicated. God's 'no' to our ability to judge, expressed in judgement upon Jesus, is God's 'yes' of vindication to us who deserved that judgement.

Let me finish this chapter in this way. I love films. I think it is *Karate Kid II* in which Daniel Son is given a classic car by the old Japanese Sempei for his seventeenth birthday. Daniel Son cannot, dare not, at first believe the generosity and love of the old man to him, an undeserving, adopted, slow-witted, immature failure of a disciple. The Sempei [meaning, I think, an older, wiser one] on the other hand is in deadly earnest and is ridiculously generous in the gift of this beautiful, priceless classic car. The scene closes with Daniel Son driving off in triumph with the Sempei waving, crying, shouting his encouragement no less triumphantly. Daniel Son knows he doesn't deserve the car. The Sempei knows he doesn't deserve it. Daniel Son knows the Sempei knows he knows. The Sempei knows Daniel Son knows he knows. In and through the obedience, death and resurrection of Jesus, every such gift, every such relationship, is a foretaste, a glimpse of *the* gift. All we have to do is dare to believe it and celebrate it, and not to detract from that celebration, nor to get unnecessarily serious. Yet lest we forget the devotion and love and its cost, let us keep our eyes at all times firmly fixed on the face of that old Sempei and the tears of joy that stream down it.

9

The Tables are Turned

Now read chapter 9 of Esther, aloud if possible. When you do this you will, as I just have, notice a change in style. For scholars this raises the question of form and redaction criticism. Have more than one account been amalgamated? What was the original version? Where did the original end? Scholarly disagreement encourages me to believe that answering such questions is doomed to failure. The approach of Brevard S. Childs, who 'offers theological reflection of the text within the context of the Christian canon' in his work *Exodus* (London: SCM Press, 1987, p. xvi), commends itself as practical and obvious, and saves us a lot of fruitless effort and time.

None the less, the style has changed. The reason may be that the drama is over. The tension, pace and excitement of chapters 3 – 8 have turned into a form of reportage as the outcome, the fulfilment of all that had been ventured earlier and gained, is acted out. This seems to be the intention of our writer. While the action in this chapter is in many ways far more important than what has gone before, it seems to me that from our writer's perspective it is not exactly secondary but utterly inevitable fulfilment. The outcome is described in such straight, almost cold, irreversible terms that I believe we are supposed not only to be making the 'obvious' connections but also to be drawing the 'obvious' conclusion: the will of God will be done.

1 The Jews are no longer a minority people in the kingdom who, according to Haman, were a people whose customs

were different and who did not obey the king's laws (3:8). They are now being helped by all the nobles of the provinces, the satraps, the governors and the king's administrators (9:3).

2 The Jews are no longer fearful of revealing their ethnicity (2:10) but are feared by many people of other nationalities in the kingdom (8:17; 9:2).

3 Mordecai the Jew is no longer seated at the king's gate (2:21; 6:12) but is prominent in the palace. His reputation has spread throughout the provinces and he has become more and more powerful (9:4).

4 The Jews are not massacred under the terms of the first edict (3:12–15), but rather under the terms of the second edict (8:9–14) defend themselves and strike down 'all their enemies with the sword, killing and destroying them', doing 'what they pleased to those who hated them' (9:5).

5 Queen Esther no longer hazards her life (4:16) but now enjoys immediate access to the king, the royal confidence and his agreement to her requests (9:12).

6 The lot which had been cast for the ruin and destruction of the Jews (9:24) has come back on the head of Haman and his sons (9:25).

7 The fasting of the Jews has turned into feasting (9:17), their sorrow was turned into joy and their mourning into a day of celebration (9:22).

The point our writer is making both in style and content is made explicitly at the beginning of the chapter. When they say that rather than being overpowered by their enemies, 'now the tables were turned and the Jews got the upper hand over those who hated them' (9:1), they provide not only a title for the chapter, but for the entire book. The impossible has been made possible. The fate of the Jews has been reversed through the actions of Esther and the grace of the king. The first genocidal edict has been reversed by the equal and opposite second edict. What could never have been anticipated or expected has taken place. Everything seemed against the Jews – their fate at the hands of the evil Haman seemed to have been sealed by the king's law and all that seemed left to them was to await their fate and suffer it heroically as many of their descendants were to do. Yet a stream of coincidences, when the cards were badly stacked against them, has contrived to produce a happier outcome.

This is reported in such a deliberately matter-of-fact way that we must not miss the obvious yet incredible reversal that has taken place. The author deliberately makes the point prosaically, in such a way that we almost miss it. We are left feeling 'What else was to be expected? That's just the way it is.' If we perish, well then we perish (4:16), but that does not change the fact that relief and deliverance would have arisen even if Esther had remained silent (4:14). The chance coincidence of Esther having become queen at this time means that since Mordecai is of Jewish origin, neither Haman nor anyone else can stand against him. They come to ruin (6:13), and the Jews obtain relief from their enemies (9:16,22). Victory is inevitable and assured. Nothing could separate the Jews from their triumph and deliverance. Despite all the odds, when they seemed to be without hope, a mediator, judge, deliverer – Esther – made the impossible possible, and accomplished their deliverance through a great reversal of fortune. It seems to me that the writer describes this in this particular manner to underline the intrinsic connection between what took place in the king's inner court between Esther and the king (chapters 5 – 7) and the events of the thirteenth day of the twelfth month (9:1). The latter is inseparable from the former. The latter is in fact guaranteed by the former and no other outcome is possible. Once Esther had found favour with the king (7:3), the outcome was totally assured and irreversible. The Jewish fate, as enshrined in the law of the king, seemed irreversible. Without hope they were condemned and awaiting execution. Through Queen Esther their fate is reversed and vengeance has become vindication. Through Queen Esther the law of the kingdom is reversed and an alternative rule of life and peace is irreversibly established: 'these days of Purim should never cease to be celebrated by the Jews, nor should the memory of them die out among their descendants' (9:28).

The writer seems to me to be sitting back from the story and asking us to draw our own conclusions from it. That the tables were turned is explicitly mentioned. None of this is attributed to God; he is not even mentioned. M.V. Fox is, I believe, accurate when he says (p. 247; I quote in full):

> When we scrutinise the text of Esther for traces of God's activity we are doing what the author made us do. The author would have us probe the events we witness in our own lives in the same way. He is teaching a theology of possibility. The willingness to face history with an openness to the possibility of providence – even when history seems to weigh against its likelihood as it did in the dark days after the issuance of Haman's decree – this is a stance of profound faith. It is the willingness of the Jew to bear the responsibility that a fickle history lays on his or her shoulders, uncertain of the future yet confident that somehow [the eternal one of Israel, will not deceive] (1 Samuel 15:29).

On that fateful day (9:1) the Jews are delivered from the equivalent of the Warsaw ghetto. I calculate the 'score' (our writer does record it) as being 75,810:0 (9:6,10,15,16). Before we move on to consider this death toll and violence in more detail, let us not miss the significance of the Jewish death toll of nil. Victory and triumph are total. Assurance is complete; there is not a single casualty. Deliverance is total and all is reversed. The verdict has not been executed upon the condemned. Unexpectedly, they are completely free, delivered from certain death into life. Everything is now ready. It is indeed finished.

With the benefit of being able to read the text through the eyes of the New Testament witness to the typological fulfilment of Esther, we are more able than our Jewish brothers and sisters to see that though trouble, hardship, persecution, famine, nakedness, danger and sword (Rom. 8:35) will be the lot of all humankind under the terms of the first edict, the terms of the second edict mean that 'neither death nor life, neither angels nor demons, neither the present nor the future, nor any powers, neither height nor depth, nor anything else in all creation, will be able to separate us from the love of God that is in Christ Jesus our Lord' (Rom. 8:38–39).

But for now the text requires that we must return to the 'score' of 75,810:0. With someone as obviously guilty as Haman, surely most normal people are quite comfortable in echoing the king's sentence of hanging him on the gallows he had prepared for Mordecai (7:10). I suspect that we can pass such a sentence without too much inner turmoil or anxiety. We may even have passed over the sentence in the story with no more than the thought that Haman got what he deserved. In this chapter, however, we have 75,810 more who were not only sentenced to death but systematically executed. I suspect that we have more than a little struggle with our inner response to this, and I intend to address this now.

It all seems rather savage and uncivilized to our modern western tastes. Immediately I say this I am aware that we can easily distance ourselves from a more underdeveloped, less advanced world in a comfortable and condescending way. We can also distance ourselves rather conveniently from our own not too distant history, to which I have already referred, not to mention from the present-day conflicts on our own doorstep. We are in danger, I would say, of distancing ourselves rather too conveniently and comfortably from the personal violence, power games and sexual politics that form the sub-plot to the story of Esther and the warp and weft of our everyday lives, without our even venturing beyond our own doorstep. I am not just referring to computer games or television programmes. I am talking about the way we conduct our most personal and day-to-day relationships. I do not believe there is a difference in kind, merely one of degree, circumstance, power and opportunity.

We must not be too quick to excuse ourselves in our horror at violence and death, nor too quick to remove, at least from ourselves, the demands of justice and the penalty for our thoughts, words and actions, when we wish to retain that penalty for others. Some suffering is undeserved, some we bring upon ourselves, some is brought upon us by the direct action of others, some by accident or chance, some is the result of the structure of an unjust society. Those of us who live in democratic societies, founded on justice and equity, should be thankful, despite their many shortcomings. Those who do not live in such societies, I believe, have a desire and a demand for such justice. However, gaining this justice includes judgement, punishment and, possibly – however unpalatable it may be – the death penalty. This may be too awful to contemplate. We are then faced with a number of possible responses.

There is firstly therefore the strong desire to deny that injustice and suffering exist and to pretend that our lives and this world are perfect, despite all the evidence to the contrary. We can deny the consequences of our actions, words and lives on others and can cocoon ourselves from the worst effects of the actions, words and lives of others upon us. This is very common in the modern western world where, despite the global village of this technological age, the sense of belonging, community, identity, respect for elders and consideration of the marginalized and poor (9:22) has been largely eroded. We choose to inhabit an individualistic, private, nuclear world (in relation to both family and bomb) where not much trickles down. We are unlikely to be our brother's keeper, let alone our neighbour's, and each person looks out for themselves.

This denial or avoidance can be active and conscious or passive and unconscious. Our reality is characterized by structural injustice and personal suffering for which it is not always clear where responsibility lies. It is clear that there is responsibility and that it does lie somewhere, yet we either desire or simply allow a negative fatalism to set in – *que sera sera*, there is nothing that can be done, certainly not by me. A passive acquiescence to the status quo takes what crumbs of comfort it can along the way. This can result in happy-go-lucky optimism, and that, while not denying the mess nor even our part in it, avoids responsibility ('as long as I don't do anyone any harm … '). These well-known words come to mind: 'All it takes for evil to prosper is for good men to do nothing.'

The second response to this reality is that of the revolutionary activist who attempts to change the status quo for or on behalf of others (usually including themselves), often by violent means. As Gandhi recognized, this seems to be a necessary stage to the third response, the 'third way', the one that Jesus and Gandhi exemplified – namely non-violent submissive resistance.

The second response demands that we must feel injustice. We must respond to evil. We cannot walk by on the other side of the road; every other human being is our neighbour (Lk. 10). We must feel the anger and the compassion, and be moved to act. Suffering, injustice, malice and evil must be stopped and those responsible must be punished. The suffering of the innocents throughout the centuries, across the world, demands restitution. The first decree must be matched by the second. If the enemies of the Jews take up arms against them they only get what they deserve: death. Surely something within us cries that this should be the case? Surely, though limited in degree and kind, the law of 'eye for eye, tooth for tooth' (Ex. 21:24), enshrined in the Old Testament and passed down in the Judaeo-Christian culture ever since, is right?

At this point we must make a slight but necessary detour through the Old Testament, as fulfilled in the New, in order to appreciate fully the three responses that we are considering, as well as their context in our story: the two decrees of the king. This will enable us to gain a biblical perspective on crime and punishment, particularly murder and the death penalty, not only in this story but also in its application to the modern world. It seems to be the case that in the Old Testament the death penalty (Ex. 21:12) was part of civil law for certain crimes. This is based, paradoxically perhaps, on God's horror at murder, as every unique and precious individual is made in his image (Gen. 5:1–2).

The terms of the first decree of judgement do not merely have civil and legal implications. That might have made it possible for us, as more enlightened modern readers or indeed as Christians, to avoid their force on the particular interpretative grounds of our choice. There is a further dimension, to which our writer alludes in the statistics. When Joshua and the Israelites attacked Jericho, 'They devoted the city to the Lord and destroyed with the sword every living thing in it [except Rahab and her family] – men and women, young and old, cattle, sheep and donkeys' (Josh. 6:21). As we have already noted, it was Mordecai's ancestor Saul who, in failing to dedicate King Agag similarly to the Lord (1 Sam. 15:15), had brought about the continuing enmity between their descendants, resulting in the story recorded in Esther. It appears to be God's will that the 'innocent' should perish. We should be very wary of viewing the inhabitants of the land of Canaan or indeed anyone whom they represent as innocent. It seems to be the case that God's initial verdict (Gen. 6:7) in the time of Noah, though not to be universally executed (Gen. 6:8), finds particular application not only in the time of Abraham (Gen. 19) at Sodom and Gomorrah but in the conquest narrative recorded in Joshua. This suggests that God's instinct about the nature of humankind was correct and that those who perished were not as innocent as we might think.

I want to say in passing that the 'just war theory' based on this Old Testament view of a holy war, which has been articulated by theologians down the centuries, was applicable only in very particular circumstances and on very limited bases of time and space, and is deeply embedded within Israel's sacred history. This does not, in my view, support its widescale use as a means of justifying the indiscriminate use of almost any and every means available in the history of other nations, and particularly those that would call themselves Christian.

We are endeavouring to hold together a number of Old Testament perspectives. There is injustice and crime, which do deserve punishment. There is a 'rule of law' – for the taking of a life there is a death penalty. For some, this judgement and punishment is experienced now as a direct consequence of antisocial, irresponsible or evil action. However, according to God's verdict, all are guilty, and all are deserving of judgement. While in temporal terms it is unfair that some should experience the judgement their crime and guilt deserve when others clearly do not, none the less all will die in universal punishment for their sins. This is an unpalatable, unpleasant truth. You and I deserve punishment and death. Some avoid their punishment until the last day, either through a failure of the justice system or because their particular crime does not have civil or legal consequences. As soon as we move into the New Testament it seems to me that this becomes self-evident from the words of Jesus. He internalizes and universalizes the principle of sin in a particularly pointed, painful, realistic and ruthless way (Mt. 5:22; Mk. 7:18–20). No one can escape the verdict of guilt. All must be punished and judged, and all must die. The first decree stands. The enemies of God's people who took up arms against them received the punishment that they deserved. I appreciate that this is too strong for the taste of some, but I believe that it is in full accord with the biblical revelation of the perilous plight of humankind. The biblical revelation is totally realistic and will not allow us either to deny or avoid this reality or even to stand against the injustice of others in such a way that we can lose sight of the log in our own eye (Mt. 7:3).

Having conducted this biblical survey, we may now turn to the 'third way' exemplified by Esther. This way may be described as submissive non-violent resistance to injustice and abuse. We will discuss in the next chapter how this affects the way the people of God should live. For now I want to concentrate on the understanding of the second edict, which takes up the theme of God's covenant faithfulness to vindicate and deliver his people. This vindication and deliverance applies not only when they are the victims of the injustice and abuse of others but when they are the perpetrators. This vindication is also God's commitment not merely to his people, but in and through them to all humankind.

How can God avenge himself upon crimes and criminals deserving of punishment and death, and at the same time maintain his covenant faithfulness to Israel and all creation to deliver them from the consequences of their sin and to vindicate them (8:13)? How can he execute the death penalty, as he must, on everyone, and yet vindicate everyone? How can God go beyond the execution of the enemies of his people, knowing only too well his own covenant people's guilt, and vindicate not only his people but also their enemies? He must, in order to maintain justice, execute judgement upon all. Yet he must, in order to maintain love and hope, accomplish the deliverance of all. Jesus, the fulfilment of Esther, must not merely obtain access to the king and intercede on behalf of his people with almighty God. He must not merely reverse the law of death and accomplish the impossible: the deliverance of his people from certain doom. He must also accomplish the deliverance of their enemies and accept the execution of that judgement upon his own people who deserve it equally. In short, in Jesus God must unify the two edicts and accomplish the deliverance of all. By substituting his son in our place to be judged, receive the death penalty and be executed for the sin of all, all may equally, in him – the deliverer, judge and representative – be vindicated and raised to life. Through the gateway of death, on the last day, we who are all equally guilty shall be raised to life forever. This includes God's people as well as their enemies.

Jesus is both the prayer of humanity, the eternal drawing near to the throne of grace, and the answer to that prayer. Jesus the servant king exemplifies the true life of a subject of the kingdom. Jesus the priest offers himself as sacrifice. Jesus the judge is judged in our place.

We believe that this deliverance, this reversal has already been accomplished, despite all the appearance to the contrary. We live in this world not only under the sentence of the first decree, but under the proclamation of the second decree. In the assurance that the sentence has already been carried out and reversed in Jesus, we live between the accomplishment of this wonderful, impossible deliverance and the day when both edicts, one for death and the other for life, will be made manifest. We live like the Jews in the story, firmly embedded in the drama of chapters 3 – 8, between the historical brackets of the kingdom and creation (chapters 1 – 2) and its fulfilment in eternity (chapters 9 – 10). We live now under the banner of both edicts. We shall examine in more detail what might characterize that kind of living in the next chapter. What will characterize the lives of those who know that the verdict upon them has been passed, and yet judgement has been executed upon Jesus in their place? What will characterize the lives of those who know that the impossibility of their deliverance has already been accomplished in the death and resurrection of Jesus? What will characterize the lives of those who know the mighty reversal of fortunes has taken place and that Jesus, forever seated at the right hand of the Father, is interceding for them? It is to such a portrait that we must now turn.

10

The Third Way

I want to take up the theme that closed our last chapter. How will the lives of those whose fortunes have been reversed be characterized? This theme is introduced in chapter 10 in a variety of ways. We are reminded of the extent of the king's empire and rule (10:1), the final chapter closing as the first chapter had opened (1:1). In this way the chiastic structure of the book is used to remind us of the context of the universal kingdom. We may have been carried away with the victory and triumph of the Jews, recorded in chapter 9, but it is essential that we come down to earth. King Xerxes is the ruler of a real kingdom in a real world and, whatever the kingdom of heaven may be like, it cannot and must not be idealized. It must be rooted firmly in an earthy reality.

Mordecai had recorded the events of this small part of the history of God's people (9:20–22) and Esther had confirmed them with her own record (9:32). Now these events are recorded in the official annals of the king (10:2), giving the reversal of Jewish fortunes a degree of permanence, a degree of independent historical authenticity. The people of God are given the hope that later kings will not be as forgetful as they once had been (6:3).

The tax or tribute imposed by the king (10:1) suggests that the events of the previous twelve months – the liberality of the king at Esther's coronation (2:18) and his strange refusal to accept Haman's bribe (3:8–11), as reported by Mordecai to Esther (4:7) – have been reversed and a normal taxation service resumed in the kingdom. No longer are the leading officials (1:3) and the former Prime Minister, Haman, elevated and honoured by the king (3:1). It is Mordecai, who has been elevated and appointed at the queen's behest (8:1–2), who receives special mention (10:2–3). There is no banquet for all the peoples of the kingdom (1:3). Instead it is the pre-eminence of the Jews, whose customs are different and who are dispersed among all the people of the kingdom (3:8), which is recorded (10:3), and whose feast is remembered (9:32).

As we would expect of our author by now, no explanatory comment is made. We are left to draw our own conclusions. If our interpretation to date had been based on God's exclusive election, protection and providential deliverance of his people, then the conclusion to the book would naturally be understood as simply a confirmation of that fate. The remarkable reversal of Jewish fortune culminating in their pre-eminence is a picture of the kind of deliverance and elevation that the Jews should expect. In fact, this is what they did expect from the Romans at the time of Jesus. However, that is not our interpretation. While I do not want in any way to minimize their elevation in status, the remarkable reversal in their fortunes or God's providential care of his people, to reduce this story to one of ethnic or religious deliverance is to miss the bigger picture. This bigger picture is consistent with the narrower, and I would say more exclusive, understanding of God's covenant faithfulness to his chosen people. Yet I believe that whereas on the one hand God's covenant partner, Israel, had (according to the biblical record) consistently demonstrated unworthiness and deserved the judgement she received; on the other hand God's covenant election through Israel is as representative for all humankind. This understanding of the role of God's people as a sign or light to the world (Is. 42:6) or to serve as a kingdom of priests (Ex. 19:6) is taken up in the New Testament (1 Pet. 2:9). It suggests that there is another, deeper and more wonderful way of interpreting these few last verses of the book.

Chapter 10 is utterly realistic about the state of the kingdom. However, at the same time, through the pre-eminence of God's people and the remarkable reversal of their fortunes, there is a suggestion of an ongoing, more permanent, almost ideal position, status and role for God's people in the kingdom of Xerxes. Here is the kingdom of Xerxes: the kingdom of heaven will look like this. All peoples everywhere will be blessed through the elevation of the Jews (Gen. 12:3). God's people are truly fulfilling their purpose of blessing the nations. Their election is for the nations of the world and their elevation and blessing is to be participated in by all peoples everywhere. As Joseph under the pharaoh of Egypt (Gen. 47:13–26), so now Mordecai under Xerxes is the source of blessing to the entire kingdom, not just the Jews. This is a broader, more representative and perhaps more biblical view of the understanding that God's covenant people have of themselves, broader than that often held by Jews and Christians. Perhaps understandably the judgement of their enemies was seen by the people of God to be evidence of their deliverance from persecution by those enemies. As we have seen, while this is the case in our story, it is not the case in the person of Jesus, who died not only for God's people but for his and their enemies too.

In the book of Esther this deliverance was not only accomplished without God's miraculous intervention, but through a woman who had deliberately accommodated herself to the ways of the kingdom in which she lived. The Jews living in this kingdom had not returned 'home', they had not separated themselves from the non-Jews, and yet their difference had not prevented their deliverance. Rather, Esther's conformity to the ways and laws of the king, her submission and her service are an example to God's people for all time of an alternative way to live. But before looking at that we must reflect upon a particular oddity of this chapter – it does not mention Esther. Once again we are left to draw our own conclusions.

M.V. Fox may be correct when he says that Mordecai's promotion, though a minor matter in the book of Esther, would be significant to the official archives (p. 130). Perhaps, but would not Esther's elevation be equally worthy of official record, or at least a mention by the author of this story if not by the king's official archivist? M.V. Fox reveals, I believe, the real intention of

our author when he concludes, 'The book does not end with
Esther, her role ended when she supports Mordecai's initiative. It
is Mordecai's glory that interests the author in the epilogue,
where he praises him for his personal glory and his unending
concern for his people. Mordecai goes down in Persian history'
(p. 130).

But why did our author withdraw Esther in this concluding
part of the narrative? Our author is both realistic and true to
their representation of her as the type of Christ. What will be
important and recorded for posterity, from that day to this, will
not be the actions of powerless members of ethnic minority
groups within the kingdom, and will certainly not be those of a
particular embodiment thereof – women. History is normally
written about powerful men and the accomplishments of men
who served them. Such a historical record would not include a
woman, neither would it include Jesus.

Let us make an assumption from this point, and suppose that
Esther is the author. She does not complain about her situation
and does not draw our attention to it explicitly, as have Vashti
(1:12) and Mordecai (3:2). In accepting the patriarchal status
quo she does not deny that reality nor avoid the responsibility.
Instead she adopts a third-way lifestyle of non-violent submissive resistance which, as we have seen, receives the grace, favour
and reversal that it sought. It is not Mordecai who as 'an ideal
figure, a repository of virtues, a shining example of how a Jew of
the Diaspora should behave ... is an exemplary figure ... a stan-
dard of right behaviour' (M.V. Fox, p. 185). It is Esther.

The conclusion to the story might seem to confirm the view
that it is Mordecai who is the hero. I trust you will have been convinced by now that this is a superficial reading. I trust too that
you will have been delighted by the author's artistry in this
chapter and her commitment, even to the last, not to put herself
forward but to depend upon another for grace, favour and
success. Let us not let her and ourselves down at the last, missing
her point that as in Esther, so in Christ and so in us. Deliverance
has been accomplished through his mediation, but for now the
kingdom of God is not fully manifest. Until that last great day,

when all will sit at the banquet table at the king's son's wedding, the kingdom will be experienced through absence and hiddenness and in likeness only. Circumstances – patriarchy, injustice, the role and status and abuse of women – have not changed at the end of the book. Despite the hope, the ideal, the assurance of total deliverance and the reversal of fortune, our author is utterly realistic. The kingdom of heaven will be a hidden, non-violent yet resistant celebration of life in the midst of death until that last great day.

The commitment of so many commentators to make Mordecai the hero of the book and our exemplar seems to me to make the very point they miss: that it is the unseen, unmentioned and unhonoured servant Esther who is the hidden exemplar and type of the one to come, the Lord Jesus Christ. Perhaps this is conclusive evidence that our author is female. To miss the author's deliberate omission of the person of Esther from this chapter, when it is she who has been at the centre of the action and drama of chapters 3 – 8, and make Mordecai the hero is also to miss what Mordecai represents. He is presented consistently as 'the Jew' (2:5; 5:13; 6:10; 8:7; 9:31; 10:3). This is not incidental:

> Only foreigners who are domiciled in Israel as resident aliens are regularly identified only by their country or region of origin ... 'Uriah the Hittite' (1 Sam 11 ...) ... 'Ruth the Moabitess' ... (Ruth 2:21). Thus, the use of this gentilic as the only identification of Mordecai signals a conscious recognition of the foreign, the diaspora, status of both Mordecai and the Jewish community throughout the book ... all the rest of Israel's literature from the exilic and post-exilic periods ... have one single-minded agenda. These works are narrowly and specifically concerned with the return of the exiled leaders of the Judaean community to the ancient land of Israel and the re-establishment of the city of Jerusalem and the Temple 'as the perfect type of divine deliverance and the first sign of ultimate redemption' ... From the perspective of this agenda, the theological estimate of the exile was 'overwhelmingly negative' ... The difference between ... [this] literature and that of the book of Esther is dramatic ... [Our author

has] but one agenda ... the joy of deliverance *in the diaspora* ... (Bush, Frederic, *Word Biblical Commentary: Ruth/Esther* [Dallas, Tex: Word, 1996], pp. 312–14).

Mordecai the Jew represents the people of God living away from the Promised Land, living in exile – like living in the kingdom of heaven on earth. Mordecai acts for our author as a type of the Church undeservedly exalted by God (in the person of King Xerxes) through the mediation of the servant king Jesus (in the person of Queen Esther). The glory of Mordecai is a reflected glory, a secondary glory, a glory bestowed, undeserved, by his queen, but no less his glory and no less ours. To overplay Mordecai is to underplay Esther and to miss the true and far greater glory of those who believe in and follow in the footsteps of Queen Esther, typologically the servant of all humankind. Those who believe are the members of the holy communion – the broken, blessed and distributed body and blood of Christ; the sign and the sacrament of the invisible present Lord of heaven and earth, yesterday, today and forever. He is present and made manifest in this world through his people, represented by Mordecai.

Having allowed ourselves to be carried away in wonder, love and praise, let us come back to earth with a detailed consideration of the likeness of the kingdom of heaven manifest on earth as exemplified in the book of Esther. The final revelation, the final reversal in Christ, will demonstrate more clearly still the intention of God for his covenant partner. The supervision of the law will be ended (Gal. 3:25), inequality will be banished (Gal. 3:28) and the slavery of the people of God will be over, for it is indeed 'for freedom that Christ has set us free' (Gal. 5:1). Ahead of time, we have in our story a partial yet unique revelation of what that kingdom might be like in the person and work of Esther. Her absence from the last chapter of her book is best understood in the light of her similarly absent type – Jesus. His way, his kingdom and his person are made visible through those who follow him. What characterized Esther will characterize his people and the kingdom.

- First, the kingdom will be exemplified in those who follow the example of Esther and adopt what I termed in the previous chapter 'the third way'. The first way, which seeks to deny responsibility and avoid reality, will not do, and neither will the second alternative of civil disobedience, exemplified in Vashti and Mordecai. The third way is that of submissive non-violent resistance to injustice. This is nothing if not realistic, as we have seen. It is not concerned with its own honour, but that of others; not with its own rights, but those of others. It is not prepared to close relational doors, but to put the responsibility fairly, squarely and definitely where it deserves to be: at the feet of the oppressor. This is not done in a hard-hearted, bitter or angrily unforgiving way, but out of an anger at injustice that is prepared to self-sacrifice and ultimately to forgive.

We see a remarkable modern-day example of this way in the life of Gandhi. I was particularly struck when watching the film *Gandhi* by the scene in which he is led into court for trial on a charge fabricated to enable the authorities to imprison him legally, yet immorally. Everyone, including the judge, stood. This third way may end in great personal self-sacrifice, persecution and even martyrdom in its refusal to compromise truth, freedom and the right and equality of all. This is because most people in power (whether institutional or personal) will feel accused, ashamed and angry at having their power and status threatened as their heart, motivation and abuse of others is laid bare for all to see.

Esther, in taking the third way, risked such a response, and Jesus experienced its consequences to the full. As he taught and lived out God's love for all – and particularly for the marginalized, frail, abused and sinful; the least, last, little and lost – he experienced the anger, hatred, malice and murderous intent of those whom he most threatened: those in power, with money, status, influence and authority. He submitted himself to the Father's will and to the authorities. He took the towel and washed the disciples' feet, making it visible that the third way of the Son of Man was to seek and to save the lost

(Lk. 19:10), to suffer and die and be rejected (Mk. 8:31) and not to be served but to serve (Mk. 10:45). The paradoxical kingdom of reversal created in so doing is one in which the first will be last and the last first (Mk. 9:35), where unless we enter like little children we will never enter (Mk. 10:15), and where whoever wants to be great must be the servant of all (Mk. 10:43).

- Second, this kingdom will be exemplified by free gift, not by duty or legal requirement, and by loving voluntary response, not by obedience. It is only *after* the Jews have established the custom of giving (9:19) that Mordecai writes to establish the practice (9:22). It was not in obedience to Mordecai's authority or command that the Jews established the custom, but because they 'took it upon themselves' (9:27). It is not because of religious obligation or Levitical requirement that Purim is established, but because of the feasting and joy that spontaneously broke out as a result of deliverance (9:17–19). It is not because of the authority or status of Mordecai that the Jews do all this, but out of gratitude for all that Esther, unmentioned at the end of her book, has accomplished (9:32).

The kingdom of heaven is characterized by free response, not legal requirement; by trusting relationship, not filial duty; by spontaneous community gathering, not religious obligation; by joy and rest, not anxiety and fear. This has all resulted from the grace and favour of the almighty ruler being extended to Esther, and from Esther to her people (5:2–8). Grace, not law. I do not believe that this is set over and against the covenant or sacred history of God's people, itself founded upon that same grace (Deut. 7:8), but alongside it. It was often the case that Old Testament religion became empty or oppressive. This secular narrative of the deliverance of God's people should have removed once and for all any danger of a religious urge for codification, for this leads to a return to slavery. Jesus too, in his life and his teaching, will demonstrate that the kingdom is exemplified by joy (Lk. 15:7,10,32), feasting (Mt. 22:1–14) and gift (Mt. 25:14–30) and not misery, duty, fasting and law. Jesus will finally put an end to such religion. What the Church throughout its history would do is, of course, entirely another matter.

- Third, this kingdom will be characterized by celebration and joy. Though I have already touched on this above, I wanted to make it a separate point because it is so significant in the book of Esther, and so important and quickly lost. Jesus' favourite image for the kingdom was a 'party'. Jesus was criticized for so often eating with the wrong sort (Mk. 2:16), the final revelation of the kingdom is a marriage feast (Rev. 19:7), and the heart of our experience of the kingdom before that day is in the celebration of the Last Supper, which we do in remembrance of him until he comes again (1 Cor. 11:24–26). Though one might not suspect as much if most church services were anything to go by, the kingdom is to be characterized by this same celebration.

We celebrate – that is, we sit at table with and participate in – the coming together of the two decrees in the person, teaching and work of Jesus. We celebrate the present reality of that first Good Friday when Jesus, the judge, was judged in our place so that we might be set free. We celebrate the present reality of that Sabbath rest of God and, in the burial of Jesus, the new creation not just out of nothing, chaos, confusion and disorder, but out of death. We celebrate the present reality of that first Easter Sunday, the resurrection to everlasting life. We celebrate that in him, Jesus Christ, our deliverance, our reversal of fortune has already 'happened'. We celebrate these truths, in the words of *The Book of Common Prayer*, 'at all times and in all places yet most chiefly when we assemble and meet together, to give most humble and heartfelt thanks for all his goodness and loving kindness to us, not only in creation and all the blessings of this life, nor even just for his providential ordering of all things for those who love him but above all, for his inestimable love in the deliverance of the whole world through our Lord Jesus Christ and for the means of grace and for the ultimate hope of glory' [my précis, extracted from Evening Prayer and Thanksgivings].

- Fourth, this kingdom celebration is not only the focus for the at-one-ment that Jesus has made for us with God by his death and resurrection, but also an expression of the peace and communion we have with one another. Throughout this book there are collective references to the people of God of the Diaspora. They are the one people, the Jews. However, unity, community, giving, consideration of the poor (9:22) and solidarity are at the heart of this communion and this celebration. All ages, all types, all perspectives, all shapes, all sizes, all classes are all equally welcome. All may draw near, all may eat and drink till he comes, all may participate in the deliverance he has accomplished and given to all freely, generously and unconditionally. As he has shown us, so we are called to love one another. The people of God are not an exclusive club with conditions of membership. The people of God are to be a sign of God's unconditional love for all humankind. The people of God are to exemplify this love to one another and to their neighbour so that only those who exclude themselves may not draw near to the throne of grace, the Cross of Christ, the table of communion.

- Fifth, this kingdom will be made visible to those who have eyes to see (Mk. 8:18). Anything and everything that some might have thought would have availed has not, does not and will not. This is a community of faith alone, of those who have come into something of the self-awareness, the realization, the revelation that all have sinned, all have fallen short, all are condemned under the first decree and yet miraculously all are delivered, freed and exalted undeservedly and by grace under the second decree. It is a community of those who, having glimpsed the grace and mercy of God, know assuredly that nothing they might do, think or feel earns them entry into the kingdom. Nothing they can do will maintain their status therein and, most fundamentally of all, nothing they do would have denied them access in the first place or would continue to deny them access. It is a community of those who believe that this deliverance has already been accomplished, despite appearances, and that this deliverance is universal in its scope and is not a religious preserve or cul-de-sac for the private enjoyment of a chosen few. It is a community of those who believe that God has not promised – and we should not expect – that we shall be preserved in the best of circumstances, any more than he has promised to deliver us from the worst, but that he has promised to be with us. This community believes that even if we perish, and often in a variety of small but significant ways part of us does, we have been and will be delivered. It believes that ultimately it is only through perishing, through the gateway of death, that deliverance, reversal of fortune, life and resurrection may be experienced. It is not deliverance 'from' nor even deliverance 'through', but deliverance 'out the other side of', into a new creation that we celebrate, often despite appearances, by faith. This new creation results from third-way living. This community is made up of those who believe that ultimately the grand metanarrative of all history, of all creation, is not religion but relationship; is not miraculous intervention but providential over-ruling or rather underpinning. It is on the underside, at the bottom of the drainpipe, that we will encounter the everlasting arms that have been there all along.

- Sixth, this kingdom is one whose reality is characterized not by choice and alternative but by tension and coexistence. It may have seemed that I have overemphasized the perspective and world view of our writer and downplayed what I have termed the more sacred view of the other writers of biblical history. If I have done this, it is only to make the point forcibly. It seems to me that they must be held together, and I believe I have endeavoured to do that as we have explored together the various ways in which Esther is a type of Jesus who also fulfils all other biblical types. Thus the non-interventionist God of Esther who will not deliver Jesus from the Cross will intervene the other side of death in the miracle of the mighty resurrection of our Lord Jesus Christ. The non-religious, non-liturgical revelation of the book of Esther is fulfilled as much in the incarnation of the Lord who eats and drinks with tax collectors and sinners as it is in this same priest, prophet, king and judge, the sacrifice, word and heir judged in our place, who is now seated at the right hand of the Father. This book that is silent about prayer portrays in the person of Esther and in her approach to the king the very heart of prayer and so encourages us to be continuously prayerful in all we do, think and say. This book points us to God, to heaven and to the covenant by portraying the likeness of the kingdom on earth and inviting us to make our own personal response of faith. Ultimately this book encourages us to believe not that we are either condemned or delivered, not that we are either members of the chosen people of God or not. We are either Jew or Gentile, but we are all of us, always, living in the light of the not yet. We are all of us always, everywhere, both condemned under the first decree and delivered under the second decree. We are all both unclean and clean (Mk. 7:19–23). Ultimately the judgement, the vengeance, the righteous anger of God falls upon the judge – the deliverer Jesus – and not us. In that same Jesus the vindication of all humankind is declared. The people of God, the community of believers, are only the first fruits of all those who have already been delivered and who will be raised on the last day, when the kingdom will no longer be visible to the eyes of faith alone and experienced only in part, but will be fully manifest to all and we shall know as at present we are known.

- Seventh, this kingdom will be characterized by growth, development, movement, accomplishment and a sense that all is well in any event – whatever happens, it is finished. While this is a particular example of the previous point, I wanted to make it a separate one, partly to make a total of seven points and in order to underline the reality that the king is always the king (1:1; 10:1). Though the Jews may be – for now, anyway – elevated, they will assuredly be humiliated again. Though they may have been delivered from death, there will occur in their history the awful reality of non-deliverance and genocide. While superficially circumstances have changed for now, ultimately history demonstrates not development, evolution and growth but – through a pattern or cycle of the rise and fall of one kingdom replaced by another – the dreadful, seemingly irreversible determination or commitment of humankind to self-destruction and the drainpipe which is its history.

At one and the same time it is also the case that, even if it is a brief break in the clouds, circumstances have changed. There is possibility, it is worth hazarding one's life, living the third way, serving others, demanding justice, living in the communion of the at-one-ment where all is not lost, or rather all has already been lost and yet found. In the end the at-one-ment typologically in Esther and in Jesus demonstrates that grace has been and will be sovereign over judgement and life will prevail over death. Therefore new life in the midst of death, in the sure knowledge of death in the midst of life, is worth living. Let us indeed celebrate!

You will not have missed the fact that I have chosen to present the above characteristics as usual in seven points. The points themselves are arbitrary and others could have been added, but I trust they all issue from the story itself. In no sense do I want to suggest that I have a complete understanding of the revelation of the book of Esther, but I do believe that Esther does. Any attempt to draw out the characteristics our author seems to me to present ought, I think, to honour not only her content but the form of her presentation.

So, by way of conclusion, I want to attempt to provide a parallel representing these seven characteristics in the form of a chiasm focused specifically in the person, character, work and accomplishments of Esther herself. This will centre upon Esther's role as the servant of God, 'the' archetype of God's self-revelation in Jesus Christ.

- First, then, as Esther freely submitted to the patriarchal society in which she found herself, specifically to the word of her guardian Mordecai (2:10,15,16), and exemplified the attitude of the Lord Jesus (Phil. 2:2), she is a pattern for all who would follow in his footsteps.
- Second, Esther refused to put any confidence in herself (4:16), her position as queen (4:11), her ability (4:16) or even her

obvious sexuality (2:17) and placed herself in complete dependence upon the grace and favour of another (5:2), the ruler of all the earth (1:4). As such she exemplified that obedience of faith that characterized Jesus, who prayed 'not my will but thine be done' (Mt. 26:39,42,44) and who is the pioneer of our faith (Heb. 12:2). She is thus once again the exemplar for those who believe.

- Third, as Esther expressed her submission obediently to both Mordecai (2:10) and Xerxes (2:8) she offered non-violent resistance to injustice and oppression and exemplified the third way of Jesus, who did not merely hazard his life (4:16) but gave it up so that those who would follow him might take up their cross and lose their life if they want to save it (Mk. 8:34,35).

- Fourth, Esther demonstrated the heart and commitment of one who refused to serve or think only of herself (4:14) and exemplified that which would be made explicit in the teaching of Jesus: 'whoever wants to become great among you must be your servant, and whoever wants to be first must be slave of all' (Mk. 10:43–44). God's servant would be made yet more wonderfully manifest as the one who 'did come not to be served, but to serve, and to give his life as a ransom for many' (Mk. 10:45), *the* servant of God (Is. 52:13 – 53:12) and the one whom those who believe are called to imitate (Phil. 2:5).

- Fifth, not only does Esther exemplify the righteousness of life described above, but she also typologically becomes the righteousness of God. As she takes on royalty (5:1), gains access to the throne of the king (5:2), receives the king's grace and favour (5:8; 7:3) and the granting of her request she exemplifies the one who was not only the Son of Man (Mk. 2:27–28) but also the Son of God (Mk. 1:1) and who in being in himself the righteousness of God (Rom. 3:21–22) draws all humankind to himself (Jn. 12:32).

- Sixth, not only does Esther in her submission and obedience of faith represent our humanity to God, and in her royalty represent God to her people, she actually and completely accomplishes her purpose in the deliverance of those people, reversing their fortunes (9:1,18), turning death (3:13) to life (9:5) and vengeance to vindication (8:13). Just as her people represent all humankind, she is a type of the Christ to come who will accomplish this at-one-ment once and for all (Rom. 5:19).

• Seventh, as Esther and her people celebrate their deliverance in perpetuity (9:28) and continue to live – despite this deliverance – in political, economic and social circumstances unchanged in the likeness of the kingdom of heaven on earth, so the people of God continue to celebrate that reality with the body and blood of Jesus, through whom, with whom and in whom we draw nearer to that day when 'There will be no more death or mourning or crying or pain, for the old order of things [will have] passed away' (Rev. 21:4).

Thus as a submissive, dependent woman, Esther exhibited the obedience of faith in the world. As the exemplar of God's servant she gained access to the throne of grace and became his righteousness for all, eternally present to the world in the mystery of the communion of the people of God.

What more perfect type of Christ is there in the Old Testament, or what greater exemplar of his way?

Summary

The structure of this book has followed the ten chapters of Esther, with their own chiastic structure and focus, and now concludes within its own doublet by way of epilogue. In the two parts of this summary I want to take up the threads that have run through my exploration.

The two threads I want to interweave are the implications of the theology of the book of Esther and its cultural explication. The question we will be addressing is: How are we to live in a strange land, for now far away from home? The typology and the status of the Jewish people in Diaspora will be the subject of the first part of this summary, which will construct the skeleton. The second part will attempt to put the flesh on the bones of what this lifestyle might be like. We are entirely dependent upon the breath of the Holy Spirit, who blows where he wills. May it be his will that we in our study approach truth or elucidate an approach to the 'third way' so that the word may become flesh and dwell among us (Jn. 1:14).

I have again chosen to expand the message of Esther in two sets of seven points. I do this not merely to echo the author of Esther but, by imitating her doublet construction, to highlight the double-sided tension or paradox that she suggests – and I believe in reality is – within the completeness of the meaning of the number seven. This reality is structured around the principle of an irreversibility that has been reversed. This reality is for now incomplete in our experience, pointing to the fullness of the third day. Yet it is at the same time a complete reality for now, in the fullness of the revelation of God and his sovereign rule on earth, mediated typologically through Queen Esther.

Part 1: The skeleton

Let us turn to the first of our set of seven points. All humankind are included in God's covenant. Every one is God's covenant partner, under the umbrella of God's grace and under the dominion of God's commitment never again to destroy all life (Gen. 9:15). It is not only the puritan pharisaical separatists, nor even the remnant returning to Judaea. In Esther it is also the non-returning exiles, the Diaspora Jews, who are included within God's covenant. It is not only the outcast, unclean sinners living on or beyond the margins of the Jewish community, but 'even the dogs under the table', those beyond the pale, way outside the normal, orthodox understanding of God's election, who may 'eat the children's crumbs' (Mk. 7:28).

There is one unitary grand metanarrative in all creation and in all history – deliverance. If the sacred history records God's covenant faithfulness to his people in the face of their consistent unfaithfulness, his promise and his name and his character, then the secular tale of Esther records no less emphatically on account of his non-intervention and non-mention God's equal commitment to those Jews living in dispersion, away from home and away from the Promised Land of blessing. God will deliver (save) all his people – the separatist remnant and the accommodated non-returnees, the religious and the secular, the Jew and the Gentile – for he has committed himself in his covenant to the deliverance of, the re-establishing of a relationship with and the blessing of all humankind.

The Bible itself records, between the account of the seven days of creation and the letters to the seven churches, that the exile ends after seventy years and the gospel of forgiveness is offered seventy times seven in all eternity, not only to the twelve but to the seventy (recorded as seventy-two in the NIV) (Lk. 9:12; 10:1). The book of Esther records the events that happened between the seventh day of a seven-day banquet that culminates in the seventh year of Xerxes' reign (1:5,10; 2:16) and the account of the feast of Purim in perpetuity (9:28) that had resulted from the issue of the second decree on the seventieth day (8:9). Our story foretells, through Esther, that the accomplishment of God's covenant in the incarnation of Jesus has, despite appearances, already been established in history and in perpetuity.

Second, while some may think they have no need of a doctor, while some may think themselves righteous (Mk. 2:17), while some may think themselves neither dead nor lost (Lk. 15:32), it turned out that it was not the Pharisees and teachers of the law (those members of the Jewish remnant who believed themselves most truly to exemplify covenant inclusion) who according to Jesus were the object of God's deliverance, love and forgiveness. The reverse was true, for in order to enter the kingdom of heaven a superior righteousness is necessary (Mt. 5:20). What qualified the outcasts and sinners was their recognition of that.

If our first point was that God's covenant love embraces all humankind, then our second is that all humankind are uniquely unqualified to be the recipients of his blessing. As Paul says, 'There is no difference [between those who think themselves members of the covenant community, the people of blessing – the Jews living in Judaea or the Diaspora – and those who knew they could not be members of that community – outcasts, sinners and Gentiles], for all have sinned and fall short of the glory of God' (Rom. 3:22–23). 'We all, like sheep, have gone astray [whether we think we have or not], each of us has turned to his own way [some more obviously than others, and some with far worse consequences for others and for themselves]' (Is. 53:6).

Typologically, in the book of Esther there is only one with the power, position, status, opportunity, willingness and access to the king who can deliver her people, and we shall turn to her shortly. At this point it is Mordecai the Jew who pictures for us our own mixture of motivation, hypocrisy, self-alienation, vain pride, shame, regret and sorrow. He is seated at the gate (4:6) to the palace. Like him we await the outcome of events beyond our control; our destiny is entirely dependent upon and in the hands of another who had 'come to royal position for such a time as this' (4:14) and for whom the 'time' had indeed come (Jn. 17:1). Mordecai the Jew, away from home, alienated from the Promised Land and seemingly without hope, is seated at the king's gate. While he may have come to his senses and realized the danger in which he has put the Jews, he does not know whether it is indeed too late for him and the people he represents, in whom all humankind are represented. He is powerless, as good as dead, without hope, lost, disabled and entirely dependent upon the service of another. As in Mordecai, so in us: we are all uniquely disqualified as God's covenant partner.

Third, if our disqualification were not enough, if our representation in Mordecai were not enough, we may perhaps attempt some excuse in identifying with Haman. If we do that, we are in fact entirely without excuse. Our guilt, placing us alongside Mordecai on death row, is bad enough, but in Haman we have been executed. If in Mordecai the gallows have been built (5:14), in Haman we have hung upon them (7:9). If in Mordecai the outcome hangs in the balance and we wait at the gate (6:12), in Haman we have, like pharaoh's baker (Gen. 40:22), fully and finally received the wages and consequences of our sin (Rom. 6:23) in the execution of the death penalty. If in Mordecai we see the terrible possibility of the likely result of being left to our own devices, in Haman we see the logical and terrible consequence of the intentions of our hearts perpetrated in our death. In Mordecai we can see ourselves as victim (4:1), but in Haman we are without excuse known to God as what we know ourselves to be in our darkest recesses: malicious, selfish and evil. If in Mordecai we may, perhaps perilously, justify ourselves to some extent, in Haman, thankfully, we are undone (7:8). If in Mordecai we may feel able to dress ourselves in sackcloth and ashes (4:1), perhaps believing we may in some way affect our own deliverance and – like the servant (Mt. 18:26–28) – bargain our way out of a tight corner, in Haman we are entirely transparent, like that other servant of God. He was only too obviously, shamefully unaware of his ridiculous pretensions, despite the lack of any clothing (Gen. 3:10). It will turn out, thankfully, that someone else will dress us and lead us where by our own inclination we would never naturally want to go (Jn. 21:18).

In Mordecai we may attempt to hide from God and from ourselves; in Mordecai we may avoid the awful truth of our shadow side and hardness of heart; in Mordecai we may attempt to shift the blame away from ourselves and deny – perhaps only in part – our responsibility. In Haman we are permitted no such opportunity. All evasive tactics are foreclosed as we are starkly presented with our own image as if in a mirror in the story of Haman. A more ugly face we would not wish to see. I am tempted to lighten the load at this point by talk of the goodness of creation and of humanity or to rush ahead to our next point and our identification with the one who looks back at us (Jas. 1:25). I must resist all such urges for I know myself too well. I suspect that you too would immediately grasp the straw of hope and deliverance before fully feeling the desperate, awful, tragic, stark, naked truth not only of our deserved disqualification from God's covenant, but also of our equally deserved receipt of the consequence of that disqualification: judgement in the form of death.

So, our second point was that we have not only been found wanting, but that we are all uniquely disqualified to be recipients of God's blessing. Our third is this: all humankind have rightly been condemned and experience the wrath and judgement of God against sin and unrighteousness, for which the sentence is death. My destiny, your destiny and the destination of all our stories is the drainpipe that history appears to suggest and that we all suspected it would be all along. But – and thankfully there is a but – our fourth and central point in the light of the foregoing is God's grace, never to be understood as cheap (Dietrich Bonhoeffer) but only and always as amazing (John Newton).

As Nehemiah rebuilt the walls of Jerusalem, so Esther incarnated the very redeeming presence of Yahweh not in the holy city but in the capital of the heathen world. As Daniel went to his room, turned his face towards Jerusalem and prayed for the miraculous intervention of God for the sake of God's name and God's covenant, so Esther went to the king's harem and the king's bed and went into the king's presence unbidden. Through her very intimacy with him the necessary intercession for her people was made, based on trust that there is a providential possibility that God will invisibly and indirectly accomplish his purpose. As Moses the prophet confronted the pharaoh and led the people of God out of slavery into the wilderness and yet failed to enter the Promised Land, so Esther submitted to the king, mediated the deliverance of her people from death and succeeded in bringing the blessings of God upon them in that very wilderness. As Joseph was sold into slavery and found himself in prison falsely accused, only to become the Prime Minister of all Egypt and the deliverer of his people, so Esther entered the king's harem, found herself, though innocent, under the sentence of death and yet as queen accomplished the deliverance of her people. In continuity with Israel's sacred history, in fulfilment of the patriarchal covenant promise succeeding where Moses failed, and acting as priest–queen, Esther is the charismatic judge, the deliverer of her people, the harbinger of covenant grace and the epitome of the servant of God.

All humankind are covered by God's covenant, the revelation of God's one grand metanarrative of all history – deliverance through reversal of fortune. All humankind in Mordecai the estranged Jew have fallen short of a covenant response of faithfulness. All humankind in Haman, the embodiment of evil, have received the judgement they deserve and the execution of the death penalty. It is also the case that all humankind in Esther have gained access to the throne of grace, have been reconciled with God and one another and themselves and have received their covenant inheritance. If in Adam (representatively Mordecai or Haman) all humankind die, so in Christ (representatively Esther) all humankind are made alive again (Rom. 5:17).

As Esther submits (2:8), resists (4:16) and serves (5:4), so in Christ we have the example to imitate (Phil. 2:5). As in Esther access is gained to the Lord of all the earth (5:2) so in Christ the Temple curtain is torn from top to bottom (Mt. 27:51) that all might enter in (Heb. 9:12). As Esther alone approached the king (5:1), so Christ alone is qualified to enter the Holy of Holies once and for all (Heb. 9:24–26). As Esther took royalty upon herself (5:1), so Christ the servant king and no other could dare to approach almighty God (Heb. 10:19–20). As Esther finally defeated Haman (7:7), so Christ has finally beaten Satan (Lk. 10:18). As Esther exalted Mordecai the Jew (8:1–2), so Christ raises all to the glorious inheritance of the children of God (Rom. 8:17). As Esther's and Xerxes' will is one and their intimacy complete (8:4), so Christ, his word and work complete, is seated at the right hand of God (Heb. 1:3). As Esther made intercession, mediated and stood between Xerxes and her people (5:1), so Christ reconciles us with God. As Esther makes the impossible reversion of the irrevocable law reality (8:8), so Christ alone makes deliverance, impossible to men and women, a reality. As Esther brings life where there was only death, so Christ makes the at-one-ment of all things for everyone always.

Our first point was that God's covenant, based on his faithfulness and his name, cannot be revoked and must be fulfilled. Our second and third points were concerned with the universality of our disqualification from that covenant and judgement under its terms (the first decree). Our fourth point was the impossible reversal of our fortunes through the mediation of Esther, typologically Jesus, alone (the second decree). Our fifth point is the at-one-ment made between decrees one and two, between God's covenant faithfulness and our covenant unfaithfulness, between God's righteous indignation and our judgement and God's love and our forgiveness, between our death and our life and – most mysteriously of all – the at-one-ment within God himself. Esther, the type of Jesus, lifts the curtain slightly into the Holy of Holies, and reveals in her person and work the very heart of God. Only one is uniquely qualified to present the acceptable sacrifice so that men and women might be at peace with one another, themselves and God, and so that there might be reconciliation between the righteous demands of God's justice and his love for all creation. Only one could make such an at-one-ment. Praise God for Jesus.

God's word of judgement, it turns out, is a word of life. God's will, it turns out, is Satan's – our death, that beyond the grave, on the other side of death, is life. Death has indeed lost its sting. It has become a gate, a door through which all will enter into life everlasting. Satan's word, 'you won't die', is God's last word. God, it turns out, isn't the awful party-pooper we've accused him of being all this time. The eternal party, rest and home, for which we all yearn, has already begun. We merely wake up to that reality either now through a foretaste of death or when we physically die. God's vengeance (upon Jesus Christ crucified), it turns out, is his universal word of vindication (8:13). The tables truly have been turned. Believe it, for if it is the case that all 'have turned away' (Rom. 3:12), it is equally true that all 'are justified freely by his grace' (Rom. 3:24). It is not just that 'all Israel will be saved' (Rom. 11:26), but all humankind. The one man who represents the way that leads to death is not Moses but Adam, and the one man who represents the way that leads to life is not Jesus the Jew only, but Jesus the Son of Man, the Son of God who wonderfully has not only entered through the gate of death for us but has become that very gate so that all may enter if they will only dare to believe (Rom. 3:22). We have only to dare to believe that all has already been accomplished for all; that the score really is 75,810:0. Total victory is assured; there are no casualties. The impossible deliverance, the impossible reversal of fortune, has been accomplished for all.

This deliverance, based on God's universal covenant and equally universal grace, is not an offer that at some future date will be foreclosed. This offer is not made to the 'elect' only – unless we understand all humankind to be that elect or chosen of God. It is not made only to the pharisaical, separatist, pure, religious, moral minority in our midst. It is a blanket offer to all, good and bad, for all 'fall short of the glory of God' (Rom. 3:23). This offer of life everlasting issues from the husband's heart for the adulterous wife (Hos. 3:1) and from the father's heart for both prodigal and pharisaical sons (Lk. 15). God's grace, God's love, God's forgiveness, God's vindicating judgement truly is his last word on our ridiculous, jumped-up, awful, unfaithful,

painful turning of our back on him. It isn't that we have merely
turned our face away and he maintains his face towards us, or
that the tables are turned, nor even that he has sought us out and
found us. It is that in our very deliberate wayward selfishness we
stumble over and into him, if we will only have eyes to see, if we
will only believe, always and everywhere, the word made flesh.
That word is ever present, yet absent, abiding invisibly in our
midst. Ultimately the everlasting arms are open underneath us as
we stumble, still blind, into the tomb of our death only to find
that the stone has already been rolled away. If we were able to
believe and trust that this is true, we might celebrate even now;
but, true to type, we continue with our candle in the dark, our
eyes tight shut, blind to the dawn. Oh that those who have
glimpsed the glory of God, tasted the goodness of God and been
surprised by joy might more faithfully be the sign, the sacrament
of Jesus and the gospel of deliverance.

Now for a cautionary word. I am well aware that many will
find this universalist talk unpalatable, not only because of their
desire to see others punished and their desire to be rewarded both
for their effort and their denials, but also because of the apparent
judgementalism of the New Testament (not just the Old) and
especially of the words of Jesus.

If God's judgement and the sentence of death pronounced on
sinners seems tough, then what of his judgement upon grace
spurned? This, I believe, is what the New Testament calls the
second death (Rev. 20:6–14). It is not, however – as Robert
Farrar Capon demonstrates in his trilogy on the parables – that
we have been baited with grace only to be beaten firmly with the
stick of judgement. That would be to have turned the good shepherd into a big bad wolf who waits at the end of time, or of our
days, ready to pounce if we have not 'believed'. God's grace
remains forever sovereign and the gate from death to resurrection and life is eternally open. We will either stumble through it
in those losses, rejections, hurts and mini-deaths of life, or when
we die. We will sooner or later be surprised – no, amazed – by
the realization of faith: that we have already been found, that
we have everywhere and always been safe on the shepherd's

shoulders and even now we are on our way home, rejoicing. But we may, God forbid, refuse to enter, refuse grace. God will allow us, however awfully for us and for him, this freedom and so there will be some whose own self-exclusion from the eternal feast will be a second death. But, as Capon suggests, perhaps God may have a 'final solution' wherein even the second death will turn out to be a second opportunity. I for one hope so, but I'm not confident. I may add that if the life of Jesus is anything to go by, then it seems to me that the most likely candidates for the second death will not be the sinners, outcasts, vulnerable and poor, but the self-righteous, religious, rich, moral leaders in our midst.

We have already begun to touch our sixth point, which is this: to the eyes of faith, God is visible always and everywhere. The Church is a collection of those who have seen something of God's goodness, tasted something of his grace, of those who gather thankfully, dependently, and for mutual encouragement to celebrate the sacrament of his mysterious presence manifest in his absence, his powerful presence manifest in weakness and his invisible activity manifest to the eyes of faith in apparent non-intervention and inactivity. It is not only the good that become an icon or window to God, but also the bad; not only the reversal of fortunes, but their non-reversal. Our deliverance has finally, ultimately been accomplished – not by Jesus coming down from the Cross, but by his remaining on it; not by his removing the gateway of death, but by his passing through it; not by his merely living under the threat of judgement, but by his drinking of the cup to the very dregs; not by his hazarding his life, but by his broken body being laid in the tomb and, of course, by his mighty, glorious resurrection therefrom and his even more glorious ascension and intercession at the right hand of God, for and with us all.

Thus to the eyes of faith, Christ and his forgiveness, his deliverance and his presence are always and everywhere available to all. This is true not only in the best of circumstances but, paradoxically, more often, more freely and more evidently in the worst. It is the poor who are blessed, the grief-stricken who are comforted, the meek who will inherit the earth and those who hunger and thirst who are satisfied (Mt. 5:3–6), not the rich or powerful (Mt. 19:22–24). It is not just that our deliverance itself is a great reversal, but that our very appreciation of it is also a reversal.

The story of Esther suggests that providence, luck, coincidence and fate are the very milieu of God's inactivity and 'absence' in his world. In Jesus it would appear that it is not merely when the very stuff of life turns out for the best but when it turns out for the worst that we may see God. We truly can have our cake and eat it, or perhaps I should say bread, broken yet blessed.

Our seventh and final point is that the experience of this deliverance is equally available to all who believe in the here and now. It is certainly not limited to a religious or a moral minority or indeed to those with much faith determined to believe in the miraculous. It is for all, not through the sacred, but in the secular; not just in the good, but in the bad as well; not just when our experience is that of deliverance, but even when it is the opposite; not just when God seems evident, obvious, present or visible, but also and perhaps more usually when God is absent and invisible.

All may give thanks for the goodness of creation and its many blessings. All may give thanks for God's providential care and provision for us in the circumstances of life, health and home. All may give thanks for the jam-side-up roll of life's die, for the coincidences that have punctuated all our lives, for those many occasions when it just so happens that things turn out favourably, unexpectedly. None need resort to the miraculous intervention of God to 'prove' his covenant love for all, or worse, his covenant love for the few who fulfil a particular and sometimes bizarre set of religious conditions. None need remain on the outside; all may draw near. None need remain in the crowd on the edge; all may reach out and find themselves not merely touched but embraced. None need feed on crumbs; all may sit at the king's table. None need fast; all may feast. Indeed, one day all will, if we could but dare to believe the amazing, comprehensive, universal grace of God.

All may likewise see the reverse of his goodness – the bad luck, those unfortunate coincidences and those jam-side-down experiences – as the paradoxical, mysterious presence of God manifest in the broken body of Jesus, the only source of true blessing, still faithful against the odds and despite appearances.

The number of us who will draw near, who will enjoy this blessing, this vindicating judgement, this forgiveness, this foretaste of the eternal party would appear – in our culture anyway – to be few. My suspicion is that in a culture that views strength, power, wealth, success, independence and status as its goals, and which is able to deliver many of these to many of its members much of the time and enable the 'unlucky' ones to live in the hope of the same, this will continue to be the case. It is my conviction that the truly lucky ones are the real no-hopers, the down-and-outs, those who in weakness, loneliness, pain, hurt, vulnerability, loss and failure taste death and thus find themselves at the gate to the kingdom of heaven. If only those who have tasted and glimpsed this kingdom could dare to share their experience of it in a form in keeping both with that experience and the gospel itself – namely vulnerability, frailty, weakness and dependence. If only they could stop believing marketing theories and selling out to the way of the western world. I am convinced that then many would be enabled to let go of the pretence that our culture holds before us and fall into the everlasting arms. I don't have much confidence that they will.

We seem to be desperate to avoid hitting the brick walls of life. If we do hit them, we certainly want to avoid hitting any more. When describing our experience to others, we describe it in a way that either turns it into a success or an achievement. How wrong this is. All may draw near on the same basis – his grace. All may enter through the same gate – death. All may experience his blessings at his table to the extent that they are the broken body. They may feed on him and drink his cup. This was never going to be a popular offer, except to the desperate. For most of us, sadly, freedom from desperate loneliness will only fully and finally dawn in death, when with all humanity we experience the gospel of God's reversal of our circumstances in all its power and all will be made alive (1 Pet. 4:6).

Part 2: The flesh

In the first part of this summary we addressed the question of the status of the Jewish people in Diaspora in the light of the typology of the main characters and plotline of the Esther narrative. I attempted to argue on the basis of that typology (i.e. through the eyes of the New Testament) and a theology of covenant that not only are all Jews, returning or not, included within God's covenant, but that all Gentiles too are to be found under the umbrella of God's grace. I attempted to argue that the very nature of the covenant is grace to and for an impossibly, irreversibly, incorrigibly unfaithful people who are only special or 'elect' in so far as they represent the character and status of all humankind. I attempted to argue that as in Adam, so in Israel and thus so in Jesus, Son of Man and Son of David. All are under the judgement of God, all are exiled from the land of God's blessing, and all live away from the Temple – the symbol of God's presence in the midst of his people. Yet despite this, despite the determination of God's covenant partner to continue in unfaithfulness, in and through Jesus the impossible has been made possible. As God's judgement has been executed upon Jesus, as God's Temple has been destroyed in Jesus and God's curse has fallen upon Jesus, so in that same Jesus all are vindicated, forgiven and raised. All are forever blessed because of God's grace and the obedience of faith of Jesus, who alone was good enough and who at this very moment is making intercession for us all.

This second part of the summary aims to take up the theme of the previous paragraph: God's universal covenant of grace with all humankind. It is time to put flesh on the skeleton of that covenant, to draw out not only its implications but its explications, with particular application for a postmodern western culture. To answer the question 'How are the people of God to live away from home (heaven) in a strange land (earth)?' we must first address two presuppositions by way of ground clearing and introduction. The two presuppositions are:

1 What is the link between God's covenant fulfilment in Jesus and his covenant partner, humankind?
2 What are the particular attributes of a postmodern western culture that not only make the book of Esther so relevant, but also make it seemingly unresponsive to a more 'normal', 'institutional', 'sacred' telling of the story of deliverance?

I want to tackle these two presuppositions in reverse order. You will probably already know the direction in which I am headed. I appreciate that I will be guilty of some generalizing tendencies, and have no detailed, demonstrable sociological ground upon which to stand. What I have to say will appeal to some, however, and it seems to me that a general instinctual feel for where we might be at is often not far from the truth. In any event, you have complete liberty to disagree and dismiss some or all of what follows. I refer back to the introduction and the world of Diana, Princess of Wales. Our culture does have a spiritual hunger. Our culture, though definitely not religious – it would never dream of looking to the Church for an answer, let alone the answer to the question of how to live – has a heart, needed to grieve, needs to be touched and is desperate to reach out. Our culture, perhaps fairly, has a view of the Church, the institution and the people of God that is, in my view, a million miles away from what I have been trying to outline in this book. I believe that this is the burden of the author of Esther. People have inoculated themselves against the 'normal' approach of religious Christianity (though paradoxically, if not surprisingly, some are peculiarly vulnerable to the approaches of other religions).

I do not believe that Christianity is supposed to be a religion. In fact, I do not believe that Esther is a 'religious' story or that Judaism was intended to be a religion. Rather I believe that the basis of Judaism and Christianity is the covenant, the invitation into a relationship with God and one's neighbour of love, acceptance, forgiveness, mutual support and consideration. As such, it seems to me, the burden of the book of Esther is peculiarly relevant to our culture, a culture that is devoid of and desperate for real relationships and real community and suspicious of and rightly cynical about organized religion. It is not only the religious tendencies of those within organized religion – so off-putting, in my view, to our author – but the equally definite religious tendencies of those outside organized religion that together form a formidable barrier to God's gracious invitation to life, love and celebration.

By religion I mean not merely its form. Ultimately, it seems to me, form is a matter of personality – (in)formal, (dis)ordered, (un)structured – some prefer spontaneity, confusion, freedom and others the security and knowledge that nothing changes. Some are temperamentally more comfortable with an awesome, holy, fearful, transcendent God and others with an intimate saviour and friend. This may be given theological, ecclesiological or even Christological clothing, but it seems to me it is largely sociologically and psychologically determined. What I mean by religion is the tendency, the motivation and the inner determination which will find expression in a plethora of forms. Some of these we would describe as obviously religious and some not. It encompasses the need to justify oneself, to prove oneself worthy – if not in absolute terms, then at least in some achievable or measurable form, gaining a pass mark over and above others. Very few people I meet are atheists (when the chips are down, anyway), yet equally few are Christians. In the terms defined above, most (perhaps all) are religious. Though they are certainly not church attenders, they want finally to know whether they did deserve to be saved – whether they were good enough.

If this presupposition, as generalist as it is, is in any way an approach to our cultural reality, how may it be reached, touched, and brought into the possibility of relationship with the God of the covenant? How does it relate to the forgiving, accepting, reconciling grace of God who has already made the at-one-ment that our very religiosity seems to demonstrate that we hunger and thirst for? The answer is in front of us. Through story. The story of Esther is a good one. Through stories we are taken beyond ourselves, we identify with the characters, we are moved to respond, almost despite ourselves. I would say that this was the reason why Jesus told stories. In stories are all our stories. In stories we encounter both paradoxical reality, through imagination, ours and that of others, and a reality that we could only hope for, that we need not fear but may dare to believe that all will be well.

Institutional religion has adopted a rationalistic, intellectual, institutional model for its representation of the truth manifest in Jesus the storytelling mystic. Jesus seemed to delight in his ability to provoke those who had done precisely that with God's old covenant and made it a religion, who in turn seemed to delight in his ability not to make 'sense', to confuse, and to present reality (the kingdom) and truth as paradox and mystery. That this has happened is testimony to the strength of the tendency within us all to express ourselves religiously. A rediscovery of the art of storytelling and delight in story seem to me to be crucial if those in our culture are to join the celebration that even now is knocking at the door. But even more important will be the need to have some in our midst who can enable us to reinterpret our own stories in the light of history and begin to see in the everyday, the secular, the normal – in the very midst of our struggle, pain, dirt and fun – the hidden, mysterious yet none the less ever-present reality of God's covenant of grace.

We shall now turn to the second presupposition. In the light of the above, if we are all incorrigibly religious yet as such alienated from God's covenant, what is the necessary link? The answer is faith. But what is faith? It is not religion. It is not religious. It is the expression of a relationship of trust. It is faith in something, or rather someone (though for many who live by faith this someone is largely unknown, due to the stumbling block of the religious form of the Church). That someone is Jesus. It is faith that he has provided what I know I need, that he has done what I would like to be able to do myself, that he has made possible what I know is impossible, that he has made what I experience within myself as irreconcilable – at-one-ment – and that he has received what I know I deserve.

Negatively, faith is total distrust in oneself and, positively, it is complete trust in him. It is to dare to believe that it might just be true that if I reach out and touch, I will not be condemned. I will not be dismissed, I will not be rejected, I will not be made to look a fool, I will not be put to shame. I will be welcomed, lifted up, embraced, restored, forgiven, accepted and loved. It is, to use C.S. Lewis's memorable phrase, to be 'surprised by joy' and to be distressed by knowledge of oneself. It is to be drawn into the story of Jesus. It is to come to the realization that it is Jesus and to ask him to go away, yet to be enjoined as friend (Lk. 5:8). It is to experience the no of God and his yes, yet paradoxically it is to hear that yes before we hear the no and then to hear that yes again. It is to hear bells ring in heaven, not because we are good, except in him; not because we deserve to be forgiven when we know ourselves as we truly are and dare to look in the mirror, yet see him. It is all, God forbid, not because of any religious motive, form or fulfilment, but purely and simply as the unmerited gift of God's grace.

Can we, will we dare to kneel, hold out our hand and receive? For unless we can become like a dependent, vulnerable, naïve, trusting, expectant, believing little child we will never enter the kingdom of heaven. Again, much of the Church in the west, at least, seems to have lost something of its own commitment to this, so powerfully symbolized in infant baptism, when it refuses those same infants access to the Lord's table. If Jesus was committed to story he was, in those stories and in his sacramental bequest to his Church, his bodily representation of himself before his return, equally committed to metaphor and simile as the means of grace. It is through the likeness of the kingdom that we participate now in the eternal reality of the celebration, one day soon to be made visible and to be participated in by all creation, of his death and resurrection. Little children are not merely a metaphor for the access of adults; they are welcome too at the Lord's table and participate, without the cluttering of so-called 'understanding', in him who has drawn and will draw all humankind to himself.

Faith is no more than a means of actualizing and experiencing now something that we will do almost anything to deny ourselves access to, both because we are religious and because we are unutterably committed to a free-market economy and hate to be the objects of charity. It will only be when we experience what children do – when we experience vulnerability and dependence, a loss of freedom, an inability to look out for ourselves – that we will be willing or able to hold out our hand, let alone kneel and acknowledge our need. In such a culture as ours this is very difficult. It is only through story, through metaphor, that I believe this connecting link, faith, may become even a possibility.

This may seem hopeless. I may seem to be saying on the one hand that our culture, committed as it is to religion, will not draw near and that our culture, committed as it is to adulthood, cannot draw near. On the other hand the Church has presented the reality of God's covenant of grace in religious terms, so as to make it both a most undesirable form of religion and a betrayal of the one who came to put an end to all religion and call all into the freedom of God's covenant of grace. I believe that despite my hope and prayer that more might experience the celebration possible for those present at the Lord's table, the number will be few. May God forgive his Church. I am saying too that our culture is particularly resistant through history and circumstance to a gospel of God's covenant grace that can only be mediated through dependence and trust in something and someone outside of itself. This is impossible to such as us. May God forgive those outside his Church.

None the less, I do believe that God has done precisely that. He has forgiven both his Church and those outside it, and goes on doing so through the permanent access gained by Jesus to the right hand of the throne of grace. I believe – and to this we must now turn – that God does make himself available now. He does that not only through his goodness and mercy in creation and providence, but also and more particularly in those very circumstances which are not good. Those are circumstances which he does not wish, which he does not applaud, but which he does allow. More than that, he overrules them for the purpose of our deliverance. In the midst of all that is worst, most painful and most awful, we may stumble into his arms. I do not mean this happens in some sentimental, physical, visible manifestation. I mean that through faith we experience the joy, the blessing and the presence of God in the poverty, pain and absence that is our reality.

Some of us are only too painfully conscious of this painful reality. For many in our culture this painful reality is all too often subconscious, repressed and below the surface, hidden from view. If God is to be apprehended, seen, felt, known, experienced, trusted, believed in, then it can only, must only and will only be in this place, the last place we want or would think to look. Ultimately most of us cannot and will not find ourselves 'surprised by joy' in the midst of the pain. Yet most wonderfully, I believe, the door to life is Jesus' death and in Jesus all have died. When we die we will all enter through that door into Jesus' life, whether we said we believed before that point or not.

Ultimately faith will be demonstrably nothing that we can do, nothing for which we are responsible, nothing for which we can take credit. It will be none of our doing. We will one day find the unwelcome visitor at our door at a time we do not expect: we will all die. The wind blows where it will, and as we bring nothing into the world so we take nothing out. Wonderfully, remarkably, that inability, that nothing, that death is all God needs. It is his very milieu. It is the raw material of resurrection to everlasting life for all.

Thank God. Of course, if we will insist on demanding our wages, comparing ourselves to others and obtaining what we deserve, even then God will not deny us the freedom to exclude ourselves from the eternal party. But if we wake up from the sleep of death to find that the shipwreck of our lives was in fact the universal safe harbour; that the drainpipe of history turned out to be the universal home we never dared dream it could or would be; that we are already clothed in him and his righteousness; that the table is already laid and the celebration already going on;

that it is beyond all we dared hope, then how blessed we will be! How great will be our failure in not believing earlier that, despite appearances, despite ourselves, all has been accomplished in and through Jesus. Such is the wonder, the riches, the glory of grace.

We have established two presuppositions. First, our culture in its distrust and denial of religion as a means of drawing near to 'truth', 'reality' and the kingdom of heaven in its likeness on earth paradoxically reveals itself to be unalterably religious, unable and unwilling to draw near. Second, our culture in its independence, self-determination and dishonest or sub-conscious repression of doubt, fear, anxiety and need is unable to draw near and indeed is hostile to the thought, let alone actuality, of becoming childlike, trusting, dependent and faithful. We can return to the question we began this summary with, namely: 'How are the people of God to live away from home, from heaven, in a strange land, earth?'

My answer to this has once again a dual purpose. The answer is important to those who at least say they are members of the Church. I believe the answer is at least as important to those who would not say they are members of the Church. If, as I believe, the Church is the body of Christ and a primary manifestation of his presence on earth, then in so far as the Church is faithful to its calling to follow him and be like him, it is the primary means, as Israel was, of all humankind drawing near to the throne of grace. It is the answer to the question put to me by a church member when I first came to St Paul's: 'How are you going to reach the parish?' The unspoken question was how would I increase the numbers in church. It is an answer to the question of what form evangelism might take in an early twenty-first century western culture.

So for the last time we shall turn to a set of seven points by way of elucidation of my answer to this double-edged question. I shall make these statements about how those who call them-selves believers might be expected to live in the light of the Esther narrative; in the light of this deliberately secular retelling of the story of God's deliverance. These seven points will be expressed in terms of what I believe the author understood through the eyes of the New Testament (i.e. typologically) and would seek to show as 'normative' for such a people in such a world, under such a king and such an umbrella of grace. This does not mean that I deny the extraordinary, supernatural or miraculous, though I do believe that such things are by definition not every-day occurrences and are therefore not to be expected. I will seek, with our author, not only to see God in the gaps, not only to see God in the miraculous intervention, but to see God in the more 'normal' unmiraculous non-intervention. God is apparent when he appears to make himself present, visible and imminent, but just as visible in the midst of his invisibility and 'apparent' transcendence and absence.

First, this God of the covenant of grace towards all human-kind is always and everywhere present for all peoples, in all times, places and things. Through the eyes of faith he may be dis-cerned right here and now in the ordinary stuff of life. This God is certainly not for the religious only, certainly not to be located only in a certain place or at a certain time and not when we have our best foot forwards, our best side to the camera or are dressed in our Sunday best. Rather he seems peculiarly and particularly at home where and when we might least expect him to be: in the midst of messy, irritable, selfish, argumentative and loud human-ity as well as among considerate, caring, appreciative humanity. He is very much at home in our story since in Jesus God has made all history his own story. God is neither religious nor to be seen only by the elect, whether understood institutionally as priest or preacher or understood charismatically as prophet or apostle. He is always, everywhere in all things. God is not to be appre-hended or seen rationally only by the intellectual, but in the expe-rience of all, male or female, little or large, old or young, through emotions and psyche, as much as through mind or liturgy.

Everything, then, may be a metaphor of my life and my place in God's world as well as of God's presence in the world. The passing of the seasons, a funeral, a party, the dance, the dancer, a wedding, a meal, the daily round, the night's sleep, the dawn, the dream, the pain and the joy of friendship – all are sacraments; in all God is present as one who was dead and is alive again. If only the Church had eyes to see and the courage to live in this sacrament, then perhaps it might not be characterized so much by misery, duty and irrelevance. Others might want to find such a God, such a lifestyle and such a covenant of grace.

Thus, secondly, this God of the covenant of grace towards all humankind is peculiarly and particularly present in and with his people, the body of Christ, the Church. Week by week the lives they have lived day by day, participating in and drawing near to him through the many and varied sacraments of his presence, are focused as they gather to celebrate their joint participation with one another in a vital relationship in him, his covenant and his grace. Together they express their dependence upon him in song, upon their knees, with outstretched hand and bowed head, as much as in crying to him for help, listening to his self-revelation and seeking renewed commitment to go on together. As one body they seek to follow in his way of love for themselves, others, Jesus Christ and the world for which he died.

Third, this God of the covenant of grace towards all humankind will be encountered as we are a part of the world and not as we seek to escape from its reality. What I have described as accommodation, over and against separation, is the locale of the presence of God, the likeness of the kingdom of heaven on earth. This life, this world, today, here and now is for now really as good as it gets. We must indeed seize the day; we must not live other people's lives but live our lives for others; we must not live only in the past or only in the prospect of the future. We must make some kind of terms with today, ourselves and others as we and they are. We need to go to our private room to pray, yet still take a full and active part in the world; to give up the king's food and yet not appear morbid; to express our faith in the at-one-ment made by Jesus in the world in a non-judgemental way. Then not only will we be blessed, but others will too. Persecution, if that is what we seek, will follow soon enough. There is no target quite so attractive as a person who, though completely aware of the dangers and the cynicism, abuse of power and self-ishness that are obvious not just in society but in all of us, will none the less exhibit patience and kindness, who will not envy or boast, is neither proud nor envious, will not be self-seeking, will neither delight in evil nor keep a record of wrongs but who is determined to rejoice in the truth and who will always protect, always trust, always hope and always persevere (1 Cor. 13:4–7).

God is not only manifest and evident in such a way in those who believe, but also in those who do not. What differentiates the two is the believer's consciousness of both the poverty of this reflection in themselves and yet that there is a reflection, and that this is true not only for themselves but in and for all. If those who say they believe in this manifest presence of God were to see him in others, then what doors might be opened, what windows of glory. This self-understanding, this seeing of God in self, in others, in the world, always and everywhere where all life becomes a sacrament, drives us unerringly to the heart of God's self-revelation.

Fourth, the God of the covenant of grace towards all human-kind is encountered crucially, fundamentally and primarily in the sacrament of death – the bread and wine, the body and blood of Jesus Christ, the celebration of that holy at-one-ment of commu-nion. As someone said to me recently, once a symbol can be explained it loses its significance, its power. This is the focus of faith and it is a mystery. Yet all may draw near, though we dare not presume upon him or our own righteousness. Though all are unworthy so much as to gather up the crumbs from under his table, yet he is the same Lord whose nature is always to have mercy so that all may draw near to his table. This includes those with much faith, those who would like to have more, those who have come to the table often, those who have not been for a long time, those who have never been. It includes those who have tried to follow Jesus and those who have not. All may draw near, for it is Christ who invites us to meet him there. It was while he was at table with them, and so with us, that he took the bread, gave thanks and broke it. As he gave it to them their eyes were opened. They, and we, recognized him. As in the opening of the Scrip-tures, so in the breaking of the bread, their hearts, and ours, burned within them (Lk. 24:30–32).

It occurs to me that I might be in danger of misleading you so that you miss the wood on account of the trees. This whole book, its entire purpose, is to open up the Scriptures that we might see, that our hearts might burn within us. It must not be either word or elements, words or symbols – oral or visual. It must be both. Each is a completion of the other, integral to the other. The word of Esther is that we celebrate. Christ speaks to invite us to his table that we might all give him humble and heartfelt thanks for all his goodness and loving kindness towards us, not only in creation and providence and all the blessings of this life but for his at-one-ment, for his grace towards us and towards all. This is so that we might demonstrate, proclaim, follow, show our gratitude not only with our lips but in our lives, by seeking to live before him, like him and in the service of him and others. Then we, the Church, will become a sacrament, a sign to the whole world not of God's deliverance, election and love of us alone, but of all humankind. The God of this covenant of grace towards all humankind is to be found in all things, always, everywhere and by all in the world. He is to be found especially in relationships, particularly as they are focused in the holy communion, the sacrament of his invisible presence.

Likewise, fifthly, this God is manifest uniquely and wonderfully in his mysterious absence. It is not just that he is good and the world is good, but that we and the world are also corrupt and bad. Yet in his grace God is most especially present, though often seemingly experienced as absent. He is most especially a God of deliverance, though often seemingly inactive. He is most especially for us, though often seemingly only when everything and everyone seems to be against us. This is a paradox, this is a mystery, but none the less true. When we can do nothing, when our resources are exhausted in desperate circumstances, then we will be found by God. It is not only through extremity that character is built and good does emerge; it is not only out of the other side of extremity that we can see this God and his good purpose and guiding hand. It is in the very midst of extremity that we may experience both absence ('Why hast thou forsaken me?' [Ps. 22:1]) and presence ('Oh my God' [Mk. 15:34]). The life of faith truly encompasses risk, danger and adventure, and the wonder of a life of possibility and trust.

This God of the covenant of grace towards all humankind is to be seen and found in the worst as much as in the best of circumstance; in the miraculous intervention as much as in the lack of it. This God is to be believed in when he is apparently inactive, invisible and absent. On the bare word of promise then he is to be found, sixthly, in the life given over to the third way, the life of service of the king and others. If we will seek justice, give up our lives and follow him, resist abuse, oppression, violence and all manner of evil non-violently, love our neighbour, love even the least of these, boldly go where not many have boldly gone before and are committed not to the Sunday service but to the self-sacrificing service of others and of truth, then we will find that we have not only been found out and found wanting but found and brought home rejoicing. To hazard life, to lose life, to lose everything, is truly to be found. It is to know we had nothing to lose in the first place, for it wasn't ours to keep. What sort of God is this who demands that we give up that which we could not hold on to that we might receive what was already ours? What sort of God is this who meets our resistance of him with an even greater resistance so that we might be incontrovertibly, irreversibly found by him in all eternity? A child playing hide-and-seek believes that by covering their face with their hands they are hidden from sight, but at the same time cannot resist peeping. We are like that with God. If only we might peep a little more so that we and others might be found in his service, which is perfect freedom.

So, lastly, this God of the covenant of grace towards all humankind is to be apprehended or experienced in truth. This is a plain statement. An honest look at ourselves and others in this world, it seems to me, can only drive us inexorably into the loving arms of God. I never cease to be amazed not only by the lengths to which others will go to avoid the truth about themselves but the lengths to which I will go. Either I can't see it or I won't see it. Either I am so wounded and disabled emotionally and psychologically that I can do nothing other than suppress the truth for the sake of my sanity, or I'm so frightened and anxious of what the truth might be that I do everything in my power to defend myself from it.

I remember the first time I was surprised by joy, found by grace, and heard the good news 'Do not be afraid' (Lk. 1:13,30; 2:10; 5:10). There was an amazing combination of self-knowledge and knowledge that I was known yet loved for all that. My response was 'Abba, Father, depart from me for I am a sinful person,' yet also 'Son of God have mercy on me,' 'Lord, I believe – help my unbelief' and 'My Lord and my God.'

Let me finish by saying that this Jesus, this God, this grace, this word, this encounter, this kingdom, this reality, this mystery, this paradox is to be found in Jesus, in the history of this world, in your history and in mine. It is received and entered into in the stories recorded in the gospels, hence my typological interpretation of the book of Esther. The truth to be apprehended, the way to be known and the life to be entered into by all will be encountered in this Jesus. As we draw near, so we find he has made intercession for us. We may be enabled to live always, everywhere, everyday, his life in this world. We may be his intercession in and to the world, not only as we withdraw for prayer but as we live in the world as prayer; not only as we feed on him in a Sunday service, but as we experience his brokenness and blessing in ours, and as we follow his example, the example of him who came not to be served but to serve and to give his life as a ransom for many (Mk. 10:45).

Appendix

Structure and Narrative

I have become convinced that a much underestimated and underutilized key to the analysis of biblical material is chiasm. Structures are always tools rather than straightjackets and must not be slavishly followed, but it is evident to me that the book of Esther relates particularly well to this kind of analysis. I outline the structure below and have based my understanding of the narrative upon the mirror-image symmetry of the book. It has a central pivot in chapter 6 between a doublet form focused in a banquet, which is peculiarly appropriate to the book's central tenet, that of reversal. I am particularly indebted in my analysis and thought to J.D. Levenson, pp. 5–12. The chiastic structure of the book outlined below seeks to show how the first half, A–C, is reflected in the second half, A^1–C^1.

It seems to me to be self-evident that the basis of a two-day Purim feast throughout the Jewish Diaspora finds biblical justification and historical demonstration in the banquet doublet structure of the book of Esther. Which was the chicken and which the egg: narrative or practice? I do not think the answer is important and commentators differ in their view. It is incontrovertible that the feast of Purim in the Jewish calendar has been practised universally since the days of the Diaspora. This is the more extraordinary in that it is an addition to the feasts provided for in the Mosaic Law. It is even more extraordinary that it is centred on a secular story.

The fact that the feast in all its secularity is still included in the canon of Scripture is a testimony to Judaism. The fact that it offends the religious sensibilities of some is demonstrated by the many apocryphal religious additions to the text (J.D. Levenson helpfully incorporates these additions into the body of his commentary).

<u>Introduction</u>   1:1 – 2:23

($1:3 – 3^{rd}$ year – to $2:16 – 7^{th}$ year)

Aa	1:3	Xerxes' banquet for Persia	⌈	2:18	Esther's banquet – enthronement
Ab	1:5	Xerxes' banquet for Susa		1:9	Vashti's banquet for women

<u>Tale</u>   3:1 – 8:17

($3:7 – 12^{th}$ year, 1st month)

B	3:15	Haman's banquet after 1st decree
C	5:5	Esther's 1st banquet for Xerxes and Haman
D	6:11	Mordecai is honoured
C^1	7:1	Esther's 2nd banquet for Xerxes and Haman
B^1	8:17	Jewish banquet after counter decree

<u>Summary</u>   9:1 – 10:3

($9:1 – 12^{th}$ year, 12th month and forever)

Aa^1	9:17	1st Purim banquet, Persia	⌈	9:30	Mordecai proclaims banquet
Ab^1	9:18	2nd Purim banquet, Susa		9:32	Esther confirms banquet

The Persian banquets of the men (and women) are mirrored by the Jewish banquets of Purim. The writer seeks to show thereby that they have equally universal implications for the kingdom. Decree and counter-decree are celebrated by Haman and his Jewish counterparts, while the pivot of the plot is bracketed by the key players at the two banquets of the deliverer–heroine, Esther. The structure amplifies the narrative's storyline of the reversal of fortunes of the powerful and powerless through the various banquets and their participants at the beginning and end of the tale. The powerless come to power; the weak, dishonour-able ethnic minority group are publicly acclaimed; the threat of death is turned into vindication and life, and fasting into feast-ing. The irreversible law of the land is fulfilled in such a way that vengeance becomes vindication and the clearly discernible 'order' is not law but the reversal of expectation that chance (*pur*) brings.

Some ironic and amusing cameos emerge as this theme of the reversal of fortune is played and replayed. A Jewish girl, out of obedience to her cousin Mordecai, kept her ethnicity secret (2:10), unlike him (3:4). She submitted to beauty treatment and the king's demands (2:16), unlike the disobedient Vashti (1:12). Esther, having spent the night with King Xerxes, pleased him more than those preceding her (2:14–17) and became queen (2:17). Amusingly, the king – furious at the disobedience of Vashti – finds himself doing exactly what Esther wants him to do (5:3–6; 7:2; 8:8). Despite the ludicrous decree that all women should obey their husbands (1:22), all peoples find themselves subject to the decree of Queen Esther (9:32).

The reversal in status of the Diaspora Jews from the beginning of the book to its end, as well as the reversal in the status of women, is accomplished by Esther. Yet despite this remarkable change in fortune, the prescribed social patriarchal minority-abusing structure is still in place at the end of the book, unchanged. The deliverance happens without the intervention of Yahweh. There are many instances of the lack of Yahweh's inter-vention as well as the lack of any deliverance in circumstances of dire need, yet I believe this story gives us hope of ultimate, escha-tological deliverance. This narrative structure demonstrates that the grand metanarrative of all reality is deliverance. This seems to me to be manifest in:

1 The miraculous sacred history of Israel.
2 The death to life cycle of creation.
3 The psalmody of Israel (see Brueggemann, Walter, *The Message of the Psalms* [Minneapolis, MN: Augsburg, 1984]).

4 The wisdom of the ancients as taken up and incorporated by Israel in its Wisdom literature (the goodness, order and pattern of Proverbs, through the questioning, vanity, despair and doubt of the writings).

The progressive and cumulative revelation contained in the Bible seems to me to point incontrovertibly to the narrative of deliverance to be fulfilled in the person of Esther (whose name means star), who would accomplish the great at-one-ment by courageous action for her people. But like all types, her actions and achievements would go far beyond what is related. Esther extended the deliverance from returning Jews to their non-returning counterparts who had remained in exile. Jesus would extend this deliverance even to their enemies – to all the world. Furthermore, he would accomplish this, not through the death of the enemies of the people of Israel, but by laying down his own life for those very enemies.

In this little book we not only have in Esther a type of Jesus, but we have in Haman a picture of the evil one and in Xerxes a statement of the ludicrous use and abuse of absolute power through the rule of law, as a counterpoint to the sovereign almighty God. Through Esther, Xerxes lays down that power for the good and sake of her people, represented by Mordecai the Jew. Mordecai is a type of the Church gloriously and undeservedly exalted as a sign of God's covenant love to all humankind.

In my view, therefore, this book is the most wonderful typological depiction of the gospel of God's grace manifest in Jesus Christ, who was crucified for all humankind and whose deliverance is accomplished not through acts of intervention and power, but through the refusal to intervene and the laying down of power. This sovereign God allows all human beings freedom and still accomplishes his divine purpose for their deliverance.

With eyes to see, then, we can take the story of Esther and learn many lessons about individual integrity, male, female and community relationships, patterns for leadership and service, the shortcomings of law, the equality and rights of all citizens, justice, and positive discrimination on behalf of the minority in our midst. Likewise, with eyes to see and by using typology we will see a pattern of reversal in history, a metanarrative of deliverance and the invisible hand of God, whether acknowledged, sought out or not, working out his grand purpose for the good of all. Whether we find ourselves as friend or foe on the side of the powerful or powerless, the good or evil, he – through his mysterious inactivity and refusal to come down from the Cross – will mysteriously be present in his absence, not only through all that is well and good. Even more gloriously, he is present in and through all that is worst, hardest and loneliest. For this we give humble and heartfelt thanks. In the most mysterious and yet most glorious manifestations of his presence, he is to be celebrated, broken and poured out, and we who eat and drink at his table will truly be blessed and distributed, for 'Blessed are the poor in spirit, for theirs is the kingdom of heaven' (Mt. 5:3).